Hanoi Journal, 1967

Hanoi Journal
1967

Carol Cohen McEldowney

EDITED BY
Suzanne Kelley McCormack
AND
Elizabeth R. Mock

UNIVERSITY OF MASSACHUSETTS PRESS
AMHERST AND BOSTON

LC 2007017320
ISBN 978-1-55849-605-7 (paper);
978-1-55849-604-0 (library cloth)

Designed by Steve Dyer
Set in Sabon
Printed and bound by The Maple-Vail Book
Manufacturing Group, Inc.

Library of Congress Cataloging-in-Publication Data
McEldowney, Carol Cohen, 1943–1973.
Hanoi journal, 1967 / Carol Cohen McEldowney ; edited by
Suzanne Kelley McCormack and Elizabeth R. Mock.
p. cm.
Includes bibliographical references.
ISBN 978-1-55849-605-7 (pbk. : alk. paper) —
ISBN 978-1-55849-604-0 (library cloth : alk. paper)
1. Vietnam War, 1961–1975—Protest movements—United States.
2. McEldowney, Carol Cohen, 1943–1973—Travel—Hanoi—Vietnam.
3. McEldowney, Carol Cohen, 1943–1973—Diaries.
4. Vietnam (Democratic Republic)—Description and travel.
I. McCormack, Suzanne Kelley. II. Mock, Elizabeth R. III. Title.
DS559.62.U6M35 2007
959.704'31—dc22
2007017320

British Library Cataloguing in Publication data are available.

This book is published with the support and cooperation of the
William Joiner Center for the Study of War and Social Consequences,
University of Massachusetts Boston, and the William Joiner Foundation,
Boston, Massachusetts.

Frontispiece: Carol McEldowney in Vietnam, 1967
(photographer unknown).

CONTENTS

List of Illustrations vii

Acknowledgments ix

Notes on the Transcription xi

Introduction by Suzanne Kelley McCormack xiii

Carol Cohen McEldowney's Hanoi Journal

European Preparations and the Journey to Hanoi, ... 3
September 9–29, 1967
    Flies to Hanoi from Prague through Beirut, Dubai,
    Bombay, Rangoon, and Phnom Penh

Hanoi, September 29–October 17, 1967 21

    Day 1: 9/29 Friday • Arrives in Hanoi 21

    Day 2: 9/30 Saturday • Driving tour of the city; plan ... 22
        program for visit; Museum of the Vietnamese People's
        Army; evening banquet and documentary films

    Day 3: 10/1 Sunday • Museum of the Revolution; 30
        evening, Song and Dance Ensemble

    Day 4: 10/2 Monday • Hanoi War Crimes Tribunal 36
        Committee; visits to bombed sites; evening, walk around
        city, Hanoi Information Center

    Day 5: 10/3 Tuesday • Visit to evacuated factory outside ... 43
        Hanoi; Trade Union Federation

    Day 6: 10/4 Wednesday • Meeting with cabinet officials and ... 49
        Colonel Ha Van Lau about bombing; Hanoi Surgical
        Hospital; weapons exhibition

Days 7 and 8: Thursday and Friday, October 5–6. Preparations 57
and trip to Nam Ha Province; bombing damage;
underground factory

Day 9: 10/7 Saturday • Air alerts; mayor of Hanoi; 64
evening, Women's Union and East German film

Day 10: 10/8 Sunday • Museum of Arts and Handicrafts; 70
Nguyen Minh Vy of *Thong Nhat;* evening, meeting to
prepare for visit with captured pilots

Day 11: 10/9 Monday • Trip to Dan Phuong Cooperative 74

Day 12: 10/10 Tuesday • Committee on Cultural Relations 78
with Foreign Countries

Day 13: 10/11 Wednesday • Viewing of *Dien Bien Phu* at the 82
Museum of the Revolution; Mr. Ky and the Journalists'
Association; evening, meeting with intellectuals

Day 14: 10/12 Thursday • Premier Pham Van Dong; 89
evening, captured pilots

Day 15: 10/13 Friday • Departure day postponed; 101
Xunhasaba (Export-Import House); noon, banquet

Day 16: 10/14 Saturday • Peace Committee; 102
evening, National Library

Day 17: 10/15 Sunday • Discussions with Jean-Pierre Vigier 103
about weapons; Nguyen Minh of the Trade Union
Federation

Day 18: 10/16 Monday • Voice of Vietnam; Hanoi Hannah; 109
evening, night schools

Day 19: 10/17 Tuesday • Departure day; Xuan Oanh discusses 111
guerrilla warfare; drive around Hanoi; Film Cartoon Studio
of Vietnam

Reflections and the Journey Home, October 18–November 3 117
Flies home via Pacific route with layovers in Hong Kong
and Tokyo. Returns to the United States through Canada

ILLUSTRATIONS

Carol McEldowney in Vietnam, 1967   *frontispiece*

Carol McEldowney in Cambridge, Mass., ca. 1971   xl

At the Museum of the Revolution, October 1   31

Vietnamese passages with translations   33

Sketch of Hanoi districts   39

Phu Xa "Hatred House," October 2   41

Trade Union meeting, October 3   46

Delegation visiting weapons exhibition, October 4, evening   54

Tran Duy Hung, mayor of Hanoi, with Carol McEldowney
and Vivian Rothstein, October 7   65

Chart of Hanoi's governmental structure   67

Chart of North Vietnam's governmental administrative
structure   80

Sketch of village layout   81

Flowchart illustrating structure of the Journalists'
Association   84

Graph illustrating monthly income   107

Flowchart of distribution of textile goods   108

Lyrics and music of "Unity Song—Ket Đoan"   142

Sketch map of hotel's Hanoi neighborhood   144

Modern map of Hanoi, neighborhood detail   144

ACKNOWLEDGMENTS

THERE ARE NUMEROUS PEOPLE we wish to thank for their assistance, expertise, and enthusiastic support as we worked to bring Carol Cohen McEldowney's remarkable travel journal to life.

First, we thank Katherine Roberts for caring for the journal for more than twenty years in her friend's honor. Together with Jesse Diamond, Kathy brought the journal to the University of Massachusetts's Healey Library in 1997, believing that Carol would have supported the Archives and Special Collections Department's mission of serving as a repository for research materials documenting grassroots political organizations and social activism. Throughout this project Kathy and Jesse have been immensely supportive of our efforts. We hope that the publication of Carol's journal will help to honor their commitment to preserve her memory and her life's work.

The Cohen family welcomed us to their home with stories, pictures, and other memorabilia of Carol's childhood. From the first moment that we made contact with him in 2001, Carol's younger brother Gil has been a great help to and friend of this project. We especially thank him for donating to the archives copies of Carol's photographs from her trip to Hanoi. We have included several of them in this volume. Although her mother, Lucille, passed away before this book was completed, we know that she welcomed the idea that students of the Vietnam War era—young and old— would be able to read her daughter's insightful journal and perhaps reach a better understanding of the time in which she lived. We are honored that Gil, Lucille, and Michael Cohen entrusted their beloved Carol's memory to us and our work.

Along the way we have been fortunate to talk with numerous men and women who knew Carol in the 1960s and early 1970s, some of whom worked closely with her in various political groups. We are particularly indebted to her close friend and confidant Dickie Magidoff. In addition to sharing his memories of Carol, Dickie provided us with a deeper understanding of the way in which she truly lived her political beliefs. Vivian Rothstein, a fellow traveler on the 1967 Hanoi trip, provided us with invaluable documents and photographs from the journey. We are deeply appreciative of Dickie's and Vivian's assistance and encouragement. Tom Hayden read the journal and shared some of his memories of Carol, for which we owe our thanks as well.

We are also grateful to Wini Breines for sharing documents and insight from her own scholarship on both the Economic Research and Action Project and the women's movement in Boston.

From the beginning of this long journey the editors at the University of Massachusetts Press have been extremely supportive of our work and patient through the many ups and downs that have delayed it. In particular, we thank Paul Wright, who has offered his advice, his ideas, and his encouragement from the inception of this project. It was because of him that we initially brought it to UMass Press, and that decision has proved time and again to be correct.

Elizabeth Mock especially thanks her sister Patricia and her friend and retired colleague John Owens, both of whom helped with proofreading the transcription. She also is grateful to her colleague Dale Freeman, who managed the Archives and Special Collections Department while she was on sabbatical leave from the university to finish this project and who scanned the images used in the volume.

Suzanne McCormack particularly thanks her parents, Tom and Dottie Kelley, for their steadfast support of her academic career. Most important, they have been exceptional grandparents and tireless babysitters. Stephen Kelley offered his much-appreciated legal expertise in the earliest days of the project. Mary McCormack has been the best friend/sister-in-law a girl could ask for. Alexander Bloom has been an invaluable mentor, friend, and advocate for this project. Finally, her greatest debt of gratitude goes to Mark, Collin, and Ian McCormack for providing lots of encouraging hugs, welcome distractions, and comic relief along the way.

Finally, we dedicate this project to the memory of Carol Cohen McElreldowney in hopes that her words will encourage others to embrace the role of citizen-activist to which she dedicated her life. Carol embodied the notion of courage—personal and political—by giving a voice to those who felt helpless in the face of seemingly insurmountable adversity. Her spirit, we hope, will live on in these pages.

NOTES ON THE TRANSCRIPTION

CAROL COHEN MCELDOWNEY recorded her *Hanoi Journal* in a small, brown leather-covered book in her neat, clear handwriting. The transcription presented here is essentially what she wrote. McEldowney made remarkably few misspellings or other errors in the content. The editors corrected the obvious mistakes and indicated those that were not obvious errors. We also corrected some of her quirks of capitalization and punctuation.

Throughout the *Hanoi Journal*, Carol Cohen McEldowney writes about the people she met and the places she visited in Hanoi and on the journey there from Bratislava and back to the United States at the end of her trip in 1967. We have attempted to verify the spellings of the Vietnamese personal names and place-names to the greatest extent possible. In most instances McEldowney did not record the diacritics used in the anglicized spelling of the Vietnamese language. We decided to leave the text as she wrote it down. Where she used diacritics, we left them. If she did not include them, we did not add them. She also consistently used contractions and underlined words and passages for emphasis. We left these elements as we found them.

Occasionally there is material in the *Hanoi Journal* that McEldowney did not write herself but included in her journal. Among these materials is a typed transcript of an account of a meeting during the trip written by a fellow traveler which she inserted in the book. Also, there are a few short sayings, poems, or songs that were written in the journal or enclosed on inserted pieces of paper but were clearly penned by some unidentified person she encountered during the trip. We indicate this in the transcript.

INTRODUCTION

Suzanne Kelley McCormack

IN THE FALL OF 1967, Carol Cohen McEldowney, a twenty-four-year-old community organizer living in Cleveland, Ohio, embarked on a journey that few Americans would dare to take. Amidst a climate of growing domestic unrest and international turmoil, McEldowney traveled illegally to North Vietnam. As the Johnson administration sank the United States deeper into a conflict for which there existed no simple solution, McEldowney went to Hanoi to meet the enemy face-to-face, determined to understand the foe that had troubled America's leaders in Washington since the end of World War II. With an eye to history and a recognition of the significance of her journey, McEldowney documented her experiences in a small leather-bound journal. The words she wrote grace the pages that follow.

The uniqueness of Carol McEldowney's journal lies in the fact that, quite simply, nothing else like it is available in print today. Recorded daily as she experienced North Vietnamese history and culture firsthand, McEldowney's journal entries bear the important distinction of being unedited by their author. Recollections of trips by American activists to the same locale during the war were edited and published by newspapers and peace organization seeking to educate readers about their activists' missions immediately after the conclusion of their trips. Subsequently, activists' memoirs have included extensive descriptions of their time in North Vietnam, examining the experience of traveling to the heart of the enemy country through their individual perspectives and personal histories.[1] All have enjoyed the benefit of hindsight. Weeks, months, or even years after their trips, these men and women were able to focus their published chronicles on those facets that they found most useful for organizing fellow antiwar activists or, in the case of memoirs, that reflected their individual stories in the most positive light. McEldowney's journal, by contrast, provides an intimate view of an activist's thoughts and observations *as they occurred*. Through her words we bear witness to the blossoming of a sophisticated political ideology that would ultimately intertwine the struggles of poor white America with the tragedy of war-torn Vietnam.

Without question, the dominant public voices of the Vietnam War era have been male. From politicians to soldiers to antiwar activists, Americans' perceptions of this tumultuous period in our history have largely been shaped by the thoughts, words, and actions of men. McEldowney's journal offers an alternative to this perspective. Carol McEldowney first gained the respect of her fellow activists as a student organizer in Michigan. High regard for her hard work, skill, and intelligence during the years following her graduation in 1964 earned her an invitation to attend an international conference in Czechoslovakia and an offer to continue on to North Vietnam. While her journal displays only glimpses of the feminist consciousness that would mark her later political activism, it is important to remember that McEldowney recorded her observations of North Vietnam aware of the fact that she was an outsider to the conflict: a woman not subject to the military draft, not married to a soldier, and without the heartache of a brother or even a close friend serving in the war. McEldowney felt compelled to seek out her Vietnamese counterparts and learn about their experiences. She searched for glimpses of everyday life that would help her better relate to women in Hanoi and appreciate the hardships they faced during wartime. As she traveled in North Vietnam, Carol McEldowney sought a deeper, more meaningful understanding of the events of her time. Her journal provides twenty-first-century readers with a unique lens through which to study those events, enlightening our own perspective on the Vietnam War era.

Born Carol Cohen on April 5, 1943, in Brooklyn, New York, to Al and Lucille Cohen, she moved with her family to Long Island during her elementary school years. The Cohens, a working-class Jewish couple, hoped that the suburbs would offer a better environment in which their three children—Carol and her younger brothers Gilbert and Michael—could grow up. "They scraped together every penny they had and [managed] to make a $100 down payment on a house in the suburbs," McEldowney wrote later of her parents. "They'd grown up in the dirty, crowded city and wanted me and my brothers to have more space. . . . [T]hose growing up years were tight: [I] went to school with lots of rich kids and spent years being self-conscious about being from the other side of the tracks."[2]

In spite of these inner feelings of inadequacy, everyone who knew her described Carol Cohen as an exceptionally intelligent, charismatic, and determined child.[3] Carol, her mother, Lucille, recalled, was "very, very bright [and] absolutely self-motivated." In her mother's eyes she was a typical adolescent girl who dated regularly and even "did bust-enhancing exercises" in her room at home. At Great Neck South High School she excelled academically to the degree that she was offered a tuition scholarship to her choice of Long Island colleges.[4] She instead opted to attend the University of Michigan in Ann Arbor, where she enrolled in the fall of 1960 at the age of seventeen.

More than ever before, in the post–World War II era, middle-class families like the Cohens were sending their sons and daughters to college. By 1960 there were 3 million undergraduates in the United States. That number would increase to 5 million by 1965.[5] Those who attended the University of Michigan in the early 1960s were offered courses taught by faculty attracted to the school by both well-funded programs and good pay.[6] By the time Carol Cohen arrived in Ann Arbor, Michigan, students were already becoming increasingly attentive to national issues such as civil rights and nuclear disarmament. In his welcome address to the freshman class in 1960, university president Harlan Hatcher encouraged these students to take full advantage of what the school had to offer, advising them to "take [a] long look at what they expect from life before deciding how the University can best help them reach their goals."[7] Tom Hayden, the undergraduate editor of the *Michigan Daily,* commenced a four-part series on students in the United States that September, focusing on the emerging activism of young Americans as evidenced by the sit-in tactics of southern civil rights advocates and student radicals at the University of California's Berkeley campus. Citing examples from the burgeoning student-led civil rights movement in the South, Hayden argued that "the student has adopted an optimistic or exultant attitude."[8]

That fall, Carol Cohen leaped wholeheartedly into both campus and national politics. Much of her political work during her early years at Michigan was done under the umbrella of a student organization called VOICE. In addition to encouraging participation in campus issues, VOICE's earliest platform included advocating for a reduction in the voting age from twenty-one to eighteen years of age. By 1963 an expanded platform expressed the group's concern for civil rights in the North and South, protection of the civil liberties of all Americans, and limitations on military and defense spending.[9] "VOICE opposes the American obstruction of meaningful social reform in the underdeveloped nations," its platform asserted. "We recognize the need for social revolution in the third world, peaceful if possible, and urge that the United States place [its] abundant resources at [these nations'] disposal."[10] Carol's participation in VOICE led her to travel to Tennessee in 1961, where she delivered donations of food, clothing, and money to evicted black tenant farmers. Other trips with similar purposes would follow.

It was while working with VOICE that Carol Cohen met and married Ken McEldowney, a fellow group member and campus political leader. To her Jewish parents in New York, Carol's decision to marry a Catholic—and a political radical at that—was deeply disturbing. Since leaving home in the fall of 1960, Carol had given her parents much cause for worry. In addition to traveling south to participate in potentially dangerous civil rights actions—at least one of which resulted in her arrest—Carol had been in trouble on campus.[11] In the spring of 1961, for example, the Cohens were contacted by the dean of women students at Michigan, who informed them that Carol had violated dorm rules by staying off campus overnight without permission. "Her attitudes and actions suggest a pattern of behavior definitely unbecoming to a woman student within the structure of Michigan," the dean reported.[12] While the Cohens were proud of their daughter's dedication to political causes, their concern for her well-being overshadowed such feelings. Angry over Carol's decision to marry without their permission, Lucille Cohen refused to attend her daughter's wedding. "I was proud of her, but at the same time I worried myself sick over her," she lamented only months before her own death in 2002.[13]

The McEldowneys were part of a large contingent of liberal student activists at the University of Michigan who together formed Students for a Democratic Society (SDS), the organization that would become the most prominent white student-led group of the decade. In June 1962, less than a year after its founding, interested students from around the country gathered in Port Huron, Michigan, to "adopt a 'political manifesto' expressing the intellectual and programmatic outlook of the organization." According to a pamphlet they titled simply "What is the S.D.S.?" their manifesto would "focus particularly on a delineation of the concept 'democracy' as it applies in such varied realms as industrial organization, education, the arts, colonial revolution and economic development, the Soviet Union and international communism, etc. It is hoped that this will provide a much needed statement of conviction and program for the young left in America."[14] The group, organizers hoped, would "create a sustained community of educational and political concern: one bringing together liberals and radicals, activists and scholars, students and faculty."[15]

Their concerns were broadly defined: civil rights for all Americans, world peace through disarmament, a loosening of university control over students, and a lowering of the voting age to eighteen.[16] Their manifesto, however, became the foundation for the New Left ideology that confronted the American establishment—socially, culturally, and politically—through the anti-nuclear, antiwar, and women's movements of the 1960s and early 1970s. Carol Cohen and Ken McEldowney—not yet married when SDS was formed in 1961—were among those students who registered to attend the first convention in late spring 1962.[17] In the woods by Lake Huron the students put forth a written manifesto to guide their activism. The Port Huron Statement, according to its authors, was "a beginning: in our own debate and education, in our dialogue with society."[18] The document outlined the group's concerns—including student apathy, the expanding military-industrial complex, the proliferation of nuclear weapons, and domestic anticommunism—arguing: "Our work is guided by the sense that we may be the last generation in the experiment with living. But we are a minority—the vast majority of our people regard the temporary equilibriums of our society and world as eternally functional parts. In this is perhaps the outstanding paradox: we ourselves are imbued with urgency, yet the message of our society is that there is no viable alternative to the present."[19] American students were attracted to the SDS vision, and campus chapters spread throughout the United States. By 1965 SDS boasted three thousand members and more than eighty campus-based chapters across the country.[20] Carol McEldowney would later describe SDS as her "political womb," while SDS historian Kirkpatrick Sale defined the organization as a "force" that "shaped the politics of a generation and rekindled the fires of American radicalism for the first time in thirty years."[21]

By the fall of 1962 other, external forces such as the violent integration of the University of Mississippi and the Cuban missile crisis were compelling Michigan students to become more conscious of the world around them. "There was greater participation in areas other than student government," the McEldowneys wrote in a short history of VOICE. "This was spurred largely by the civil rights movement and a growing realization that a student should participate actively as well as vocally in other than purely campus programs."[22] As more Michigan students became attracted to VOICE's platform, the group became the official campus chapter of SDS, and the organization's focus again widened.[23]

In the fall of 1964, having completed their undergraduate studies, Carol and Ken McEldowney left Michigan for Cleveland, where they had agreed to work as community organizers for SDS's Economic Research and Action Project (ERAP). Living in the inner city, working alongside the poor to secure better welfare benefits from the state government, Carol saw a world in stark contrast to her own middle-class upbringing. Earlier in the year President Johnson had declared an "unconditional war on poverty in America," pledging more than $1 billion in anti-poverty programs.[24] During the spring of 1964 he toured parts of Appalachia with journalists. "Helicoptering on through Kentucky into West Virginia," wrote journalist and author Taylor Branch, "Johnson strayed from his improvised itinerary into poverty so authentic that some in his party gagged from the acrid smell of open sewage and permanently unwashed bodies. . . . Always, Johnson talked of poverty as the nation's enemy."[25] The time seemed right for significant legislation to end such suffering. According to Johnson's biographer Robert Dallek, the American public

> didn't object to Johnson's grand designs. To the contrary, his positive outlook on the nation's future was a welcome antidote to the grief and dejection so many Americans continued to feel over [President John F.] Kennedy's assassination. In short, Johnson's enthusiasm and confidence that they could reach unprecedented heights made Americans feel better about themselves. Never mind that he was overstating and overselling his vision of where he hoped the country would go. It was enough that he forecast a better day when pride in the nation's accomplishments would replace recrimination and doubt about a violent America doomed to national decline.[26]

While Johnson pushed his legislative agenda in the nation's capital, on the local level ERAP was envisioned by its founders as a link between white America and those in the black community who were struggling for equal rights. Group leaders modeled themselves after the Student Nonviolent Coordinating Committee (SNCC), young men and women demanding desegregation in the South. "The freedom movement in this country," ERAP founders explained,

> has expressed needs which will require fundamental change in America in order to be satisfied. Yet it lacks the active support of its potential allies: the unemployed whites, the under-educated youths, the aged, trade union people who know the consequences of a narrowing job market, and the many intellectuals who realize that the present

government programs against poverty are a temporary ameliorative to the crisis of economic displacement, unemployment, and automation into which we are now entering. The Negro freedom movement may face increasing isolation and frustration if it cannot soon forge links to local movements of unemployed, farm hands, displaced miners, and others who share a common economic tragedy.

It is with the conviction that new forms of economic organization, program and strategy are needed that SDS has turned major resources and energies toward a bold new task of community unionization.[27]

Funding for this "bold new task" came from corporate grants (including $5,000 from the United Auto Workers) and private donations. Chapters were started in Boston, Chicago, Philadelphia, Newark, and Baltimore, to name only a handful of the cities into which the ERAPers ventured.[28] The Cleveland chapter—known as the Cleveland Community Project (CCP)— welcomed Ken and Carol McEldowney to its ranks in the fall of 1964, after Carol's graduation with honors from the University of Michigan with a degree in political science.

Earlier that year, medical students Ollie Fein and Charlotte Phillips had laid the groundwork for the Cleveland project when they wrote to the SDS National Office (NO) asking for suggestions as to what political work they could do during their summer break.[29] In February, Carl Wittman, a recent Swarthmore College graduate, visited Cleveland and reported back to the NO on the prospect of stationing an ERAP project in the city for a summer trial.[30] By spring the NO had hired another Michigan graduate, Sharon Jeffrey, to organize the Cleveland project full-time, and in June an enthusiastic group of twelve men and women arrived in the city to begin their work. Their first projects ranged from the mundane task of painting the interior of the house they had rented at 2908 Jay Avenue to visiting with local church leaders to discuss a voter registration drive. The group divvied up the household tasks and assigned various men and women the roles of "Potatoe Keeper," in charge of planning daily menus; "Broom Keeper," responsible for directing the cleaning and fixing-up of the house; and "Treasurer," to maintain the group's scant finances.[31]

Having forged connections within the community during the summer, in September 1964 many of the twelve original Cleveland ERAPers returned to their undergraduate or graduate studies. The McEldowneys went to Cleveland to become permanent ERAP staff members. Upon arrival at the CCP, Carol took on the task of "keeper-of-the-books," a difficult job in a project starved for funding. "Present cash-on-hand (in the bank) is $330.48 which is *very* deceptive," she reported to Rennie Davis at the national ERAP office. "It includes $360.00 to pay for Charlotte's tuition next semester—so we're actually in the red."[32] The estimated budget for eight months of work in Cleveland, including rent, utilities, travel, and salaries of $15 a week for each of the five staff members, was $580 a month.[33] Carol McEldowney, therefore, wasted no time in beginning to solicit donations. "Congratulations on the $45,000 [grant]," she wrote a friend later in the month. "Though it's only half of what you wanted, the figures sound astronomical to us here in Cleveland, starving away and existing on a $300 loan." The couple planned to travel to Washington, D.C., later that fall to meet with potential donors. "Are there other people you know . . . whom we should talk to about fund-raising?" her letter continued. "Could you call such people and tell them about us and that we'll be calling them[?]"[34] Strained finances and limited funding continued to be a problem for the Cleveland Community Project beyond 1964. Writing to prospective ERAPers in the summer of 1966, for example, the CCP warned, "Anyone who joins us for the summer will be asked to try to raise, through friends, fund-raising projects, or whatever means possible, $200 to cover the cost of living and working here for the summer." [35]

Two years after her arrival in Cleveland, McEldowney joyfully wrote a friend, "It's becoming more and more frequent for us to have victories now."[36] On a political level, Carol McEldowney and Cleveland ERAP were beginning to see progress by 1966 as they forged stronger connections with their neighbors and community. Her young marriage, however, had not survived the day-to-day pressures of living and working in the project. The McEldowneys divorced in 1965, though Carol retained her married name for the remainder of her life.[37] Ken McEldowney left Cleveland while Carol stayed to continue her work organizing welfare recipients. In 1966 she took a job in the Cuyahoga County Welfare Department as a paid state caseworker to gain a better understanding of the system from the inside. Cleveland's Near West Side had no shortage of problems. "Housing is run-down, overcrowded, and expensive for the many people who rent," the CCP reported. "Other problems stem from institutional neglect and abuse: the many welfare recipients in the area live a bare subsistence and dehumanized life. . . . In brief, the problems of the Near West Side are the problems of many poor neighborhoods—physical dilapidation, social fragmentation, political neglect and abuse—where the lives of most people are governed by forces over which they exercise no control."[38]

Through her work with welfare-recipient mothers and her paid employment in the welfare office, McEldowney saw firsthand the inequities of government assistance. She retained the position just long enough to achieve an insider's perspective on how welfare was distributed. In her letter of resignation to the County Welfare Department in July 1966, McEldowney acknowledged:

> When I accepted the job I knew that welfare payments in this state are exceedingly low, that many people live on bare subsistence budgets. . . . I knew that items that many of us consider necessities, such as telephones, refrigerators, or washing machines, are considered luxuries when requested by clients. . . . I took the job knowing that I disagreed with many of the policies. And I was aware that there would be pressures on me to conform, to become more accepting of rules I felt were wrong. Even anticipating these pressures, in just over three months I have found them overwhelming.[39]

Armed with a deeper understanding of the system and a renewed sense of commitment to the struggle, McEldowney returned to focusing full-time on organizing local poor women.

During the late summer of 1966, the Welfare Grievance Committee—a group composed of ERAPers and neighborhood welfare recipients—planned a demonstration to demand a larger welfare allowance for school clothing. It had been a violent summer in the city of Cleveland, where several days of race rioting had erupted in July.[40] With September fast approaching, the group decided on a unique form of civil disobedience. "Some of us will go into May Company," a flyer announced. "We will go to the children's department; we will pick out clothing that we need for our children; we will go in groups to the cash register and ask the cashier to charge our clothing to the welfare department, explaining that the welfare department is responsible for the health and welfare of our children, which means clothing them decently."[41] The Grievance Committee's goal was to draw media attention to the inadequate amount of money welfare-recipients were given to clothe their children: "$5.00 once a year in your September check is a slap in the face," organizers wrote. "It is not enough money to buy shoes, boots, underwear, shirts, gloves, coats, and dresses. Have your children ever been embarrassed and not wanted to go to school because of their clothes?"[42] More than fifty women participated in the "buy-in" at Cleveland's May Company department store. "Five dollars," the *Plain*

Dealer noted in its coverage of the event, "wouldn't have purchased one pair of blue jeans."[43] The event succeeded in drawing attention to the problem, but definitive changes in the welfare system remained elusive.

During the spring of 1967 Carol McEldowney, along with fellow ERAPers Kathy Boudin, Sharon Jeffrey, and Paul Potter, wrote a three-page informational piece titled "Crisis in Cleveland," which encouraged members of the community to come together to improve the city. They called upon teachers, social workers, lawyers, labor organizers, and others to join in building "a broadly-based movement for change in Cleveland. Part of that movement," they argued, "means creating a 'community' within the city."[44] As President Johnson continued the escalation of American military action in Vietnam, McEldowney's personal work remained focused on organizing Cleveland's poor. In July 1967, for example, she traveled to Ann Arbor for a conference on "Radicals in the Professions." There she delivered a paper titled "The Radical and the Welfare System," in which she argued: "People who are forced to live on welfare are, on the one hand, criticized and ostracized for being on welfare, and, on the other hand, are made to be thoroughly dependent upon that same system. [The] system violates the basic democratic principle that people should be able to control their own lives and it ignores any belief in human dignity."[45] After describing her view of the welfare system as "deliberately punitive" and paternal, McEldowney concluded that a strong challenge to the welfare system had to be mounted by clients themselves. "It is only when welfare clients . . . begin to articulate for themselves what is wrong and what it is that they need," McEldowney concluded, "[that the system] will begin to change. It is only through effective political action by clients that the traditional expectations about poor people's behavior and abilities will be challenged and begin to falter."[46]

From September 1964 until she left Cleveland in the spring of 1969, McEldowney's dedication to the welfare rights movement never wavered. Thumbing through the many notebooks, journals, and letters that remain a testament to her work in ERAP, one learns of McEldowney's attendance at numerous demonstrations, meetings, and late-night planning sessions at which ERAPers and neighborhood men and women strategized over how best to deal with the state welfare authorities. Writing to the SDS National Office from Cleveland in late 1964 and early 1965, McEldowney mentioned only in passing her participation in local antiwar demonstrations. During this period she collected numerous pamphlets on the war—published by SDS and other peace-oriented organizations—and was obviously interested in learning the history of Vietnam in addition to understanding America's support for the war itself.[47] As a community organizer, however, she believed that her energies were best used at the local level, in demanding that the state and federal government make substantive economic reforms to ease the burdens of the poor. In short, while her welfare work was scrupulously documented, far less evident in her personal papers was her growing concern over the war in Southeast Asia. Reflected in the journal that follows, therefore, are the observations of a young woman committed to eradicating poverty but only beginning to understand how American foreign policy could be linked to economic problems at home.

By September 1967, when Carol McEldowney traveled to North Vietnam, American military intervention in the region required the presence of more than 400,000 troops.[48] Following President Franklin Roosevelt's death and the culmination of World War II in 1945, four successive presidents had increased the U.S. military's role in the conflict. Harry Truman laid the foundation for an interventionist foreign policy with his pledge to "contain" communism in the late 1940s. By labeling Ho Chi Minh, the nationalist leader of North Vietnam, a communist, the Truman administration justified giving aid to the United States' French allies as they struggled to regain control of their Indochinese colonies after World War II. According to historian Marilyn Young, "substantial material aid was made available to France to pursue its war against the Viet Minh, including $160 million in direct credit late in 1946 expressly for use in Vietnam."[49] Although Ho had tried to gain support from the United States for the decades-old Vietnamese struggle for independence, European alliances and a growing suspicion of communism in the West thwarted these efforts. By early 1947, the historian George Herring has argued, "the Truman administration had drawn conclusions about [Ho Chi Minh's] revolution that would determine U.S. policy in Vietnam for the next two decades."[50]

Following an intense war to quell the spread of communism in Korea, President Dwight Eisenhower's administration increased U.S. aid to the French war effort. In the spring of 1954, however, the French were dealt a definitive blow by the Vietnamese, who defeated their troops at the battle of Dien Bien Phu. Shortly after, negotiations began in Switzerland to decide the future of Vietnam. In June 1954 the Geneva Accords sought to bring peace to Vietnam, determining that the small nation would be temporarily divided at the Seventeenth Parallel and that French troops would retreat south of that demarcation line in preparation for a complete withdrawal. In the future, the accords proclaimed, no foreign nation could have a military base on Vietnamese soil. Most important, an election would be held in 1956 to determine the leader of a reunified Vietnam.[51]

Agreements at Geneva did not bring stability to the region, however. Herring has argued that at Geneva, "the major issues over which the war was fought were not settled. The terms were vague in crucial places, and different people viewed their meaning quite differently."[52] In fact, U.S. involvement in Vietnam increased after the Geneva Convention, as Presidents Eisenhower and Kennedy—refusing to abide by the rules of the accords—committed additional economic and military assistance to the regime of Ngo Dinh Diem, a corrupt Catholic brought to power with American aid in 1954. Under Diem, American advisers entered South Vietnam to provide military guidance. By the fall of 1963, however, President Kennedy—who had increased the U.S. presence in South Vietnam to more than sixteen thousand advisers—had grown weary of Diem's unpopularity among the South Vietnamese people.[53] Earlier that year Vietnamese Buddhists, who made up the majority of the population, had launched an intensely sobering protest of Diem's regime, including hunger strikes and acts of self-immolation.[54] Just weeks before President Kennedy was murdered in Dallas, Diem was assassinated in a United States–backed coup.

Kennedy's successor, Lyndon Baines Johnson, had visited South Vietnam as vice president in May 1961. According to Robert Dallek, the trip "was meant to reassure Diem and the South Vietnamese people that the United States would not abandon them to the communists. . . . On his return to the United States Johnson pressed the case for a greater commitment to the defense of South Vietnam."[55] When he assumed the presidency on November 22, 1963, there were fewer than 20,000 U.S. military personnel serving in Vietnam.[56] Within two years, however, Johnson's administration had increased that number to approximately 185,000, despite a 1964 campaign pledge to keep the United States out of war.[57] The buildup of troops in Vietnam was the result of Johnson's commitment to containing the spread of communism and his inability to see that the North Vietnamese were determined to win independence at any cost.

As Johnson increased the United States' military presence in Vietnam, opponents of his policies became increasingly vocal at home. Domestic opposition to U.S. foreign policy in Southeast Asia had sprung out of the anti-nuclear movement of the 1950s and the student and civil rights movements of the early 1960s. By 1965 such organizations as Women Strike for Peace (WSP) and SDS, both of which began in the early 1960s as responses to the growing militarism of the Cold War era, had turned their attention to Vietnam. It was, in fact, a massive march organized by SDS that first brought widespread attention to Johnson's troubled agenda abroad. In the early spring of 1965, SDS called on its members and other sympathetic parties to march on Washington against U.S. military action in Vietnam. Labeling the war in Southeast Asia a "civil war" that was "hideously immoral," organizers argued: "The current war in Vietnam is being waged on behalf of a succession of unpopular South Vietnamese dictatorships, not [on] behalf of freedom. No American-supported South Vietnamese regime in the past few years has gained the support of its people, for the simple reason that the people overwhelmingly want peace, self-determination, and the opportunity for development. American prosecution of the war has deprived them of all three."[58] On April 17, 1965, approximately twenty thousand activists gathered in Washington to show their disdain for the United States' policy in Vietnam.[59]

Carol McEldowney's Cleveland Community Project was well represented at the march by Paul Potter, the SDS president and a Cleveland ERAPer, who addressed the crowd in a rousing speech that afternoon. A month later, in May 1965, McEldowney noted to herself that organizing the local poor around antiwar issues was going to be extremely difficult. "People often assume that we support the war," she wrote, "and disagreement with that becomes the basis of [the] relationship, and often we can't move from that. People might join [us] because of shared ideas about things locally, but once they realize that we are 'communists' we've had it (and so have they)!"[60] Eager to teach the community in which they worked about the growing conflict in Vietnam, in August 1965 the CCP hosted Nancy Gitlin, who had recently traveled to Indonesia to meet with North and South Vietnamese women. "We viewed this [visit] as an excellent opportunity to talk seriously about the war with people in the community," Sharon Jeffrey wrote in the *ERAP Newsletter,* "and [to test] people's reaction to the war." The CCP brought Gitlin to meetings at homes in both black and white neighborhoods to discuss her experiences in Asia. At one such meeting at the home of a white resident, Jeffrey explained, "the women were particularly interested in what it was like over there: 'How hot is it? What do they eat? How do they dress?'" At a second meeting, also held in a white neighborhood, however, Jeffrey described the hostility with which Gitlin's presence was met:

Nancy had hardly begun, when the [female host] in a raised voice declared that if our government had decided it was necessary to fight in

Viet Nam, then that is what we must do. The United States fights only those wars which are just and moral. When we described that the U.S. was supporting a dictator in South Viet Nam, she got very angry. . . . When we showed her the pictures of the atrocities, she said that these were tactics Communists use to get the people to go against the government. . . . A couple days later we were told by another friend that [the host] said she had thrown us out of her house because we were communist.[61]

Gitlin faced similarly skeptical responses at meetings in the black community, particularly from male veterans. The visit was extremely "valuable," organizer Sharon Jeffrey wrote: "We learned a lot more about the people we're working with and about our society. This was discouraging."[62] Negative responses from neighbors to Gitlin's visit made clear to the Cleveland Community Project that much needed to be done to explain the war and its consequences at home and abroad to America's poor.

Between April 1965 and September 1967, numerous acts of individual and collective protest occurred in the United States, which sought to force the Johnson administration to recognize increasing public concern over the war in Indochina. In November 1965, for example, a Quaker named Norman Morrison committed the gruesome act of self-immolation in front of the Pentagon. Morrison's personal act of protest shocked Americans and the administration alike. It was followed in 1966 and 1967 by the formation of numerous groups of peace-minded citizens throughout the country, including Clergy and Laymen Concerned about Vietnam (CALCAV), the Student Mobilization Committee (SMC), and, most profoundly, Vietnam Veterans Against the War (VVAW).[63]

Carol McEldowney's participation in the movement was locally based until late in the summer of 1967, when she received an invitation from fellow Michigan graduate and Newark ERAPer Tom Hayden to attend a conference of radicals in Bratislava, Czechoslovakia. The Bratislava Conference, as it came to be called, brought together representatives of the American New Left with members of the North Vietnamese government and the National Liberation Front (NLF). Czechoslovakia was chosen as a central meeting point between the United States and Asia. There, approximately forty Americans met with twenty Vietnamese, representatives of both the Democratic Republic of Vietnam (DRV) and the NLF.

According to Christopher Jencks of the *New Republic,* although they represented the North and South, respectively, the Vietnamese "presented a united front in both public and private gatherings, never contradicted the official positions taken by their leaders back home or at the conference, and exercised considerable caution in saying anything to the Americans which might conceivably be used against them or their cause."[64] Among the topics discussed by conference participants were the U.S. bombing campaigns, the military, women in Vietnamese life and politics, and Buddhism.[65] As discussions concluded in Bratislava, the Vietnamese invited Tom Hayden and six fellow Americans to visit North Vietnam. In addition to McEldowney, whom Hayden had known through their work in SDS, the others included in the trip to North Vietnam were Vivian Rothstein, a member of Chicago's ERAP project Jobs or Income Now; Norman Fruchter, a filmmaker; ERAP coordinator Rennie Davis; and Bratislava attendees Robert Allen and John "Jock" Brown.

Summarizing his experiences for the journal *Christianity,* Brown, a minister, wrote:

> Some members of the U.S. delegation of which I was a member (all but me were under 30) went on to Hanoi. That we did so illustrates that in this peculiarly debasing nonwar Americans may discuss the peace movement with guerilla [sic] leaders, have the experience of being bombed on a rural bridge by the guy from the next town back home, then meet him in a prisoners' compound—all, so far as we know, without breaking any law other than a state department administrative regulation on use of a passport for "travel to, in or through Communist controlled portions" of various countries.[66]

For the seven Americans who undertook this journey—and dozens of others like them throughout the war—the experience of traveling to North Vietnam during wartime was indelible. The historian Mary Hershberger writes that Vietnam-era travelers to Hanoi and its surrounding provinces varied in age, religion, and political persuasion. "From the beginning, most of the travelers to Hanoi shared some level of opposition to America's involvement in the war," Hershberger argues.

> Some of them opposed it on moral grounds, seeing the war itself rooted in western imperialism. Some opposed it on humanitarian grounds, objecting to its cost in lives and the environment; some opposed it for reasons of history and international law, viewing the American war in Vietnam as violating the Geneva Accords signed in 1954. Some were

disturbed that, as the war progressed, the United States became ever more isolated in world opinion. They believed that waning support for the war from America's closest allies should have counted for something in Washington.[67]

In Prague days before she would leave for Hanoi, McEldowney contemplated her decision to accept Hayden's invitation. "I have thought long and hard about the reasons for going to Hanoi," she wrote on September 21, 1967, "yet I have not thought at all. . . . In Bratislava, the opportunity to go seemed the once-in-a-lifetime chance. I was convinced by the arguments of the personal effect it would have on me, the need to develop a long-range perspective on the (peace) movement, the need for community organization work to have more contact with and affect the anti-war movement. . . . Of course, the fact that the possibility arose while in the middle of a meeting with the Vietnamese whetted my desire to not only hear but to see."[68] McEldowney's journal documents the questions swirling in her head as she prepared for the journey: Could she afford the trip financially? Was her commitment to the antiwar movement strong enough to validate her having been invited? And what would her responsibilities to the movement be after the trip? Pondering these and other questions in her journal, McEldowney would eventually conclude: "There is a great need for Americans to know and understand the war, the bombing, and the society of the DRV. Conversations at the [Bratislava] conference were a beginning. But there is no doubt that actually seeing the war and meeting the Vietnamese in their own land will teach a lot more."[69]

En route from Prague to Phnom Penh, McEldowney and her companions stopped in the cities of Beirut, Dubai, and Rangoon before arriving in Cambodia on September 26. McEldowney was immediately struck by the overwhelming heat and the foreign smells:

For the first day the combination of sun and smell created faintness. (By the 2nd day I was adjusting.) Finally (and of course most significant in the long run) is the culture[,] which I am not yet sure how to characterize. In the hotel: many Cambodian boys bowing at your service, almost tripping over you; hundreds of taxi drivers (cycles) waiting to pounce; very dramatic influence of the French . . . ; miserable poverty, and a surprising degree of class difference; streets lined with Chinese, Vietnamese, and Cambodian shops, many of which also house total families who can be seen eating and sleeping on their floors.[70]

Days later McEldowney observed similarly "pungent" odors upon her arrival in Hanoi. On her first morning in the city McEldowney wrote, "Awoke early to the many noises outside—bells, bicycles, horns, but mostly the rain."[71] That day the group received an itinerary for the days ahead. Planned events included a meeting with the Vietnamese Peace Committee and the Hanoi Committee for the Investigation of War Crimes, factory tours with trade unions, visits to hospitals to meet victims of U.S. bombing campaigns, and a meeting with captured American prisoners of war.[72] The itinerary was created by Peace Committee officials responding to the requests of the seven Americans before they arrived in Hanoi. Very early in the trip, however, McEldowney realized that her visit to North Vietnam would be strictly controlled and monitored by her hosts. "It is going to be difficult to see things informally," she wrote on September 30. "Our request for 'culture' turned into an official evening of entertainment. But we are aware of the need to be insistent about some spontaneity—for example, seeing a street dance. And we have been surprised about the relatively relaxed response of the Peace Committee to our taking off alone on walks."[73]

McEldowney and fellow traveler Vivian Rothstein were pleasantly surprised when an impromptu walk on the afternoon of October 1 led to an unforgettable meeting with a North Vietnamese militiaman. "A fine thing occurred," she remarked in her journal that evening. "While we were sitting on [a] bench, a militia man, in uniform and carrying hats, suddenly stopped, walked over to us, and shook hands."[74] A crowd gathered and the women attempted to speak French and Vietnamese—the few words they knew—to the people, unsuccessfully. "I tried to explain to our 'translator' who we were," McEldowney wrote. "Hard—so hard—to say 'I am an American' in that situation. They must hate us (imagine a German speaking to Americans on a street corner during [World War II]—he would've been lynched). It was difficult to know if we were acting properly, but I think we did ok—weren't insulting, and satisfied people's curiosity a little."[75]

When the Americans met with the Hanoi War Crimes Tribunal during the afternoon of October 2, a spokesman gave the group a history of Hanoi and the damage the city had sustained. A member of the War Crimes Investigating Committee took the group on a tour of damaged buildings, including a hospital and a shopping district. Finally, they were brought to Phu Xa village, a community bombed in August 1966 but rebuilt by villagers in less than a month's time. "The People's Council and administrative committee of Phu Thuong commune . . . have constructed a monument on the spot of the house whose family of 8 was killed, and have built a 'hatred house' to store evidence of U.S. war crimes in the area," McEldowney observed. "Similar museums have been built in other parts of DRV."[76] "Trade Union Day," October 3, consisted of a visit to a factory built amidst thatched huts. "I don't know what my image had been of an 'evacuated factory,'" McEldowney wrote, "but this was not it!"[77] That afternoon, while learning about the organization of trade unions and public health organizations in North Vietnam, McEldowney saw an antiaircraft missile for the first time, which she described as looking like "white smoke streaking through the air."[78]

In the early days of the visit, McEldowney and her traveling companions were overwhelmed with information about the nation's history, the people's perspective toward the war with the United States, and the cultural traditions of the Vietnamese. What they did not know, McEldowney remarked in her journal, was much about the Vietnamese Communist Party and its role in the war. The Americans were told, for example, "that people's spirit was great because we have Bac Ho [Ho Chi Minh], the Workers Party," and "the socialist countries 'support and support of all the progressive peoples of the world.'" But, McEldowney continued, "all of us, on the trip, I think share the same uneasiness about trying to decipher the truth and figuring out how best to read between the lines of many things said. . . . It certainly is frustrating to be given 'the line' as often and as officially as we are, but we don't know if that is more a testimony to who we are and what we're expected to learn and do, or about the nature of the government."[79] As McEldowney struggled to understand the intricacies of the Communist Party in North Vietnam, she also pondered how to use what she had found out during the trip once she returned to Cleveland. "For me (for us?)," she noted, "the problem will be to learn to communicate what we've seen to people in the U.S. without seeming brainwashed by DRV propaganda but by being able to give concrete evidence."[80] These challenges were complicated by the inability of group members to speak Vietnamese.

The group traveled by caravan to Nam Ha Province the morning of October 6. "Going south, on Route 1," McEldowney wrote,

> we saw continuous destruction: repeated efforts to bomb the road and the parallel-running railroad, villages on either side, individual large buildings—all ruined. Also many shelters being built along the road. As it grew dark the frequency of trucks passed—difficult to see the contents but some were road-repair brigades, others carried machinery. Many Russian trucks; much scattered machinery in protected boxes along the route. In some cases thatched huts concealing

equipment. Crews repairing the railway. They seem prepared to jump in and repair things immediately. But what is evident is the repeatedness and thoroughness of the U.S. attacks, not their success in stopping transport and communication. Surprisingly, we saw power lines standing all over.[81]

Arriving in the province hours later, McEldowney remarked on the high level of security surrounding the group. They were taken to visit the site of a hospital destroyed by four separate bombings, where they visited with patients: "2 school kids, 2 workers," McEldowney noted in her journal. "This part of the routine makes me shudder—I really resent it."[82] Days later the group toured a model cooperative in Dan Phuong Province outside Hanoi inhabited by more than five thousand people. There they visited a school where students exhibited military-like discipline. "About 35 kids in the class," McEldowney recorded, "with 9 girls all at the back. . . . The school is surrounded by dirt walls and shelters, all the kids carry pellet hats, and some had first-aid kits."[83] Opportunities to observe the day-to-day life of the North Vietnamese people also provided the group with the chance to experience life in a war zone. "During the morning the U.S. planes keep the village busy," McEldowney wrote of Dan Phuong Province. "Between 7:30 and 8 a.m., while in the reception room, we constantly heard planes and distant bombing and kept going back and forth into the shelters, though nothing was really close. Yet it became a pain—easy to see how people are used to it and expect it, yet without question it interrupts their lives, all the time."[84]

Throughout their visit to North Vietnam the question of whether the group would meet with American prisoners of war being held in Hanoi was discussed often. McEldowney herself was uncomfortable with the idea of meeting the soldiers and expressed doubt that such a meeting would have any political relevance to the antiwar movement. A representative of the Journalists' Association called Mr. Ky discussed the American POWs with the group on October 11. From his perspective "they are murderers and by Vietnamese traditions, a 'murder can only be avenged with the life of the murderer,'" McEldowney noted. "Yet the pilots are protected with health care and better food than many of our people receive," Ky told the group. "They were walked through the streets of Hanoi so the people could see the face of a person who bombs children. Yet they were protected."[85] McEldowney would later observe that Ky's harsh words were "the first time any Vietnamese revealed with such depth of feeling the inner hostility and torture (his own word) about the captured pilots and the absolute injustice they feel at carefully protecting those who have murdered their children."[86]

The following day, October 12, the group met with Premier Pham Van Dong in the morning and three captured American servicemen in the evening. "This [meeting] was in several ways one of the shakiest, unnerving experiences," McEldowney noted. Her journal describes in detail the three young men with whom the North Vietnamese had arranged for the antiwar delegation to meet.[87] The first was Elmo Clinnard Baker, a major who lived in San Antonio, Texas, with his wife and two children. Baker was shot down in June 1967, at which time he suffered a severely broken leg. Of Baker—who at the time of the meeting was in a cast from ankle to rib cage—McEldowney wrote: "We were warned that he is still frightened; his psychology is upset because of his recent capture, and that we shouldn't ask too many questions. 'Don't shake his mental' was the translation we got!"[88] The group, McEldowney noted, were the first Americans that Baker had met with since his capture in the late spring. "Cameras didn't help," she lamented. "Although we did agree that pictures weren't to be taken during actual conversations (and they weren't), the entrance and exit pictures even made me squirm."[89]

McEldowney next described Douglas B. Hegdahl, a navy man who she noted was "very young" and "thoroughly 'discombobulated'":

He described the amazing tale of having fallen off the ship (in spite of a guard rail) in pitch black darkness, being in the water 5 hours, and finally being found by a fisherman who took him to military authorities.

A strange kid, in some way the nerviest. He couldn't keep his mind on anything for more than 5 seconds. But he did ask, at different times, who sent us, who financed us, and whether we were Communists. He also asked about the movement, about baseball, negotiations (country-by-country), [and] the presidential election. . . .

I didn't care for him particularly, was bothered by his seeming vacantness, and couldn't tell if he was playing a role or not, nor did I puzzle out the significance (if any) of Major Bai encouraging him to speak.

I did very little talking during this interview, also. (He kept rubbing his eyes in a strange, nervous manner.)[90]

Finally, the group "interviewed" an air force captain named Larry E. Carrigan from Arizona. Carrigan questioned the group's antiwar perspective and described his missions out of Udorn, Thailand. McEldowney felt no real personal connection or kinship with Carrigan. "He 'knew' we were Communists; and I knew in the U.S. he would be an enemy, a typical air force trained anti-Communist sharpie," she wrote afterwards.[91]

Beyond meeting the three Americans prisoners, for McEldowney the significance of that evening's events was linked directly to her understanding of the group's visit to North Vietnam on the whole: "I felt for the first time that we were being used by them [the North Vietnamese] for their own propaganda," she remarked in her journal later that night. "I knew that, naturally, before even meeting the pilots, but I was aware of a narrow line we had to draw—hate the pilots as I may, it is still a betrayal at the worst and unnecessary at the least (of the kinds of people we are) to be operating politically at the level of helping the Army deal with the American prisoners. . . . It is madness to assume we can 're-educate' them or tell the Vietnamese how to."[92] The group concluded from the meetings that the prisoners' health was "obviously good" and that they were living in "reasonable" conditions. When delegation leader Tom Hayden questioned the validity of some of the statements the American POWs had made about their living conditions to the North Vietnamese after the meeting, he was quickly rebuked by Major Bai, who remarked that previous visitors had had "proper opinions." In the end, McEldowney concluded, "the issue of prisoners is not a good organizing issue" for the antiwar movement.[93]

After several more days of visiting evening schools and other local institutions, McEldowney summarized: "Hanoi is like a mobile factory. All over, every street, are many humming little shops: some have generators, some repair bicycles, but all over the sense of motion. Feverish motion."[94] The group had a final "formal meeting" with the Film Cartoon Studio of Vietnam, an institute that created cartoons for children. "In general," McEldowney noted, "all who see the cartoons are educated about revolutionary heroism and the importance of education." Cartoon topics included patriotism, discipline, honesty and bravery, and hygiene.[95] "I felt like the films were too moralistic in ways," McEldowney acknowledged in her journal, "yet interesting, and I wish I knew how representative they are of other educational forms and how they're greeted."[96]

The group departed Hanoi on October 17 and traveled through Laos to Phnom Penh, Cambodia, via commercial airplane. As she prepared to leave

Southeast Asia, McEldowney considered the significance of the customs she had observed in Vietnam, including the selling of flowers in the markets and the formality of tea ceremony rituals. Among "other impressions," she noted "the noises of the city—they begin early, 5:00 a.m., with a myriad of bell bicycles, some car horns, and occasional loudspeaker announcements. . . . In the streets, the bicycles have competition from the numerous small humming machines, all sizes and shapes, and from the sound in places of construction work. Some people hawk their products on the street, but not many or at least not very noticeably. I was struck by how much the noise is that of work, rather than of play and entertainment."[97] McEldowney recalled the vast assortment of posters and other propaganda she witnessed in Hanoi, in sharp contrast to the lack of written material evident in Phnom Penh.

The seven-member American delegation parted company on their way back to the United States. Four members of the group headed to Paris, while McEldowney traveled via Thailand and Hong Kong to meet with students in Tokyo. "No doubt that we've shared a unique experience," she noted, "not likely to recur. . . . [W]hen will I ever go 'round the world again???"[98] McEldowney filled several pages of her journal with reminiscences of the journey, including the sights and sounds of Hanoi and Phnom Penh. Arriving in Bangkok, she was struck by stark signs that the U.S. military had a strong presence in the small nation. "First transit stop: Bangkok. A terror of an experience," McEldowney remarked. "A huge, spanking new, American-financed airport, absolutely crammed with expensive goodies to buy. Many U.S. planes (fighter bombers) on the airfield, many Americans inside; an English-language newspaper for the U.S. population. . . . American presence was simply overwhelming, just at the airport."[99] Arriving in Vancouver, McEldowney felt an awkwardness upon her return to the West. "Strange to be here," she noted. "Miss Hanoi, but anxious to see American friends and test my knowledge, ability, effectiveness. And hastily finish writing before it passes."[100]

The last pages of her journal were dedicated to the task of reflecting on the political and emotional value of the trip. The entry for October 30 begins, for example, "An attempted summary. . . ." Over the course of several days and a dozen or so handwritten pages, McEldowney attempted to reconcile her feelings toward the trip, the Vietnamese, the U.S. government and military, and her fellow activists. Among the problems McEldowney saw with activists' traveling to Vietnam was the language barrier. "Short of learning Vietnamese (which no Westerner really does well because of all the accents), one cannot avoid talking through an interpreter," she reasoned. "That raises a variety of problems. First, learning to find out when the translator understands you and when he doesn't. Second, it's easy to talk to the translator rather than the non–English speaking person, instead of seeing the translator as a 'means.'"[101] McEldowney described feeling "overwhelmed" at times when she could not communicate directly with those she met during the trip. In addition to the language barrier, McEldowney was equally struck by the significance of cultural differences. "To begin with," she explained,

> the country of Vietnam is alien on several levels: it is an Eastern country, with a different philosophical/religious tradition . . . ; it is a socialist society which makes its structure, government, way of doing things quite unfamiliar; and perhaps hardest to comprehend, it is a society at war. . . . It is impossible to conceive of constant expectation of death, yet everyone in Vietnam is well aware that in the next day, week, or month, the possibility of death for a close friend or relative is real. Within moments, an air alert may take people out to their defense posts—and bombs may fall! (Yet the irony is that often we were very shielded from the reality of the war, certainly from death.)[102]

As she sought to come to terms with the significance of her trip to Vietnam, McEldowney tried to identify lessons she had learned that might be carried over into the antiwar movement. "Vietnam," she argued, "now suffers greatly as the object of the American war. What happens there is the result of American success or failure; very little regard is paid to the strength of the Vietnamese as their own agents."[103] Like many of her fellow Americans who ventured into this unknown and potentially dangerous locale, Carol McEldowney returned to the United States determined to share what she had learned with others, be they students, activists, or skeptics. Her journal, therefore, stands today as a lens through which we may better understand travel to the North Vietnamese war zone as a unique form of protest undertaken by groups of dissenting Americans for a multitude of reasons. For Carol McEldowney, at the heart of this journey was a desire to learn: a determination to understand both the people of Vietnam and the conflict that was tearing apart the very fabric of American society in the 1960s.

In February 1973 the journalist Andrew Kopkind tried to make sense of the political and social upheavals of the previous decade in an article titled "The Sixties and the Movement," which appeared in the radical journal *Ramparts*. By "movement" Kopkind referred to "a single, if shadowy, integrated political consciousness that could embrace the ideas of blacks and whites, women and men, First and Third Worlds, straights and gays, students and non-students."[104] In his piece, Kopkind chronicled the birth of the student-led New Left, its connections to the movements for civil rights and against the war in Vietnam, and its demise "into bitterly antagonistic factions" by decade's end.[105] For Carol McEldowney, living communally in Boston when the article appeared, Kopkind's words opened a floodgate of memories. "Reading [Kopkind's article] . . . just made me cry," she lamented: "i'm not sure why, in the way, sometimes, i cry about my life. the tears aren't sentimental—i agree with Andy that dialectics deny nostalgia. perhaps i cry because the decade is done and i am a child of the 60s. some of my tears are shed for friends who are dead, others for friends missing in action. i am neither yet i cry for myself as well. the pain: the passing of what's familiar, the unknown of the future."[106]

McEldowney's personal history was punctuated by the major events of the 1960s. In her days as a student activist at the University of Michigan, her academic life was intertwined with her political beliefs, leading her to participate in civil rights actions in the South while simultaneously increasing her understanding of the Cold War and international events. In the years that followed her graduation in 1964, she ventured into a world radically different from that of her middle-class upbringing in order to help those less fortunate. In Cleveland she witnessed the inequities of capitalism: boys and girls who lacked adequate clothing for school; mothers who could not afford to feed themselves or their children, let alone pay rent on their dilapidated apartments; men and women who had blind faith in their government's actions abroad despite the injustice of the welfare system that (barely) supported them at home. Just as Carol McEldowney tirelessly championed the cause of Cleveland's poor, she undertook an equally complex political challenge as her country's involvement in the war in Vietnam escalated. As McEldowney's journal of her trip to Hanoi indicates, seeing the war from the perspective of the Vietnamese—America's "enemy"—was an invaluable learning experience. "I had expected to see a country 'going under,' gradually giving in to the immense pressure of the war," she wrote in February 1968. "But during my visit I encountered an attitude toward independence and revolution that reminded me of the descriptions of American patriots during our own Revolution."[107]

Reflecting on her journey later that same year, McEldowney told a close friend: "There was tremendous personal risk in that [trip]: what might happen to us, where would I go and what to do afterwards? and I was pretty scared by it. But I realize now that the risk and the unknown opened up lots of new possibilities, creative ones."[108] Immediately after her return from North Vietnam, McEldowney began visiting college campuses to speak about the war and her observations of the North Vietnamese people. These campus engagements only created more questions in her mind: How, she wondered, could her trip to North Vietnam be used as an organizing tool to amass more support for the antiwar movement? "First, when I returned," she wrote in November 1967, "I felt that anti-war organizing was the obvious thing to do. . . . But now I'm not so sure of that."[109] McEldowney expressed ambivalence about her future role within the antiwar movement in correspondence to friends and political comrades throughout 1968, becoming increasingly critical of the movement in the days following the outbreak of violence at the Democratic National Convention in Chicago.[110]

In May 1969 she left the largely dismantled Cleveland Community Project and moved to Boston. Shortly before leaving Ohio, where she underwent nearly five years of intense politicization in some of our nation's poorest neighborhoods, McEldowney typed a four-page essay she titled "A Personal Manifesto . . . of sorts . . . thoughts about the movement," which explained her political views at that time, including the questions that she believed had yet to be answered by the political movements of the 1960s. "We must choose," she concluded: "Do we build the American revolution, rooted in the common people of America, where they are? Or do we assume that students are the revolution, and others will fall in line? The choice is clear to me. If the revolution we want is one that will create a democratic, anti-elitist, anti-manipulative society, we must build it, from the grass roots up."[111] In Boston, amidst the backdrop of a growing movement for women's liberation and an increasingly violent and radical antiwar movement, McEldowney continued to expand her personal and political horizons. Working with local antiwar organizations, however, she became more and more disillusioned with the direction of the mostly male-led movement. After a protest on the campus of the Massachusetts Institute of Technology in November 1969, for example, McEldowney expressed concerns about her place within the movement of which she had so long been a part:

> I felt the awful contradiction: all of the stuff I have learned from the women's movement was being sucked out of me. To be heard, to make a dent on the politics of the thing, I had to be tough, superarticulate (and

just as militant as thou!), aggressive, angry, competitive. Ugh. So much of that part of me has softened as I've learned to trust and like other women, to cooperate with them, to dig seeing lots of people being leaders and not needing the leadership position for myself. Yet the draw was incredible—I felt what was happening, knew it was bad, yet couldn't bring myself to say fuck it and leave. Lots of the women who went through this together talked at great length later, purging ourself.[112]

Although McEldowney continued to espouse an ardent antiwar ideology and to participate in demonstrations—including organizing antiwar GIs in South Carolina in 1970—increasingly her political focus became women's liberation. McEldowney allied herself with an emerging Boston-based women's organization, Bread and Roses, and studied martial arts, penning a chapter on women's self-defense for the groundbreaking first edition of *Our Bodies, Ourselves,* a first-of-its-kind women's health resource published in Boston. In 1971, just shy of her twenty-eighth birthday, McEldowney began compiling "The Coming Out Journal"—a binder of letters, notes, and poetry dedicated to her developing awareness of lesbianism and her realization, after many failed heterosexual relationships, that she was gay. In March of that year McEldowney participated in the takeover of a Harvard University building by several hundred women demanding that the structure be used for a city women's center. "The presence and participation of many gay women was . . . [a] crucial factor for me," she wrote in her journal. "I guess I'd been a closet case for a while and the women's center created space for me to come out. Coming out is partly a public declaration for other people, but its greater significance is as a statement of self-acceptance, yes, self-love, that I feel good enough about being at a certain place that I want my friends to accept that as an integral part of me."[113] McEldowney's subsequent political actions and ideology were largely guided by this important realization.

Responding to Andrew Kopkind's article on the movements of the 1960s, McEldowney was inspired to think about her personal history. "i want to understand . . . where i've been, and where i'd like to be," she reasoned. "who i am and how i got to be that way. it feels like an ocean, the ebb and flow of movements."[114] During the summer of 1973 McEldowney traveled west from Massachusetts to California, meeting friends and former political allies along the way, seeking to understand her own metamorphosis. As with so many of the events of her remarkable life, a handwritten journal documents McEldowney's journey west. "I'm going on a trip to reconnect with my past," she wrote excitedly before leaving Boston.[115] Tragically, her life ended abruptly during her return to Boston. After more than a month of visiting friends throughout the country, Carol McEldowney died in a car accident on September 5, 1973, at the age of thirty.

The war in Vietnam, and the movement against it, would drag on long after McEldowney and her six fellow travelers left Hanoi. In the spring of 1968, President Lyndon Johnson succumbed to negative public sentiment about his handling of the war and announced that he would not seek reelection. President Richard Nixon's first term in office witnessed efforts to negotiate and settle the conflict, clouded by an escalated bombing campaign and the expansion of the war into neighboring Cambodia and Laos. Domestically, an organization of Vietnam veterans grabbed the public's attention by marching on Washington to demand a withdrawal of all American forces from the region. Finally, in January 1973, a peace agreement was reached. The people of Vietnam, however, would continue to live under a dark hailstorm of war as fighting continued between northern and southern forces until the North's ultimate victory in April 1975. Throughout the 1970s the Vietnamese remained at war with Cambodia, causing further bloodshed and death.

Traveling to North Vietnam in 1967 offered Carol McEldowney the opportunity to experience a culture entirely foreign to her own. There, amidst fears of being bombed and frustrations over her inability to communicate effectively, McEldowney recorded in vivid detail observations of her nation's "enemy." She witnessed the hardships wreaked upon civilian schools and hospitals, acknowledged the resolve of the North Vietnamese military and government to defeat the United States, and respected the determination of the people to survive this terrible period in their history. Returning to the United States, McEldowney sought ways in which to use the information she had acquired in North Vietnam to gain public support for the antiwar movement.

As time passed, however, McEldowney's ideology, like the political issues that so affected her life, grew increasingly complex. At the time of her death in 1973, the war was no longer her most pressing political concern. Ever evolving with the times in which she lived, McEldowney, like many politically active women of her day, embraced the goals of women's liberation, linking the political demands of women to the other causes that she had so emphatically championed. The trip to Vietnam provided Carol McEldowney with the opportunity to identify with the Vietnamese in a way that the majority of Americans could not: as people, not a faceless enemy.

Carol McEldowney in Cambridge, Massachusetts, circa 1971 (photographer unknown).

It also allowed her to witness the imperfections of the political movement with which she was so closely allied, to observe her fellow activists' words and deeds as they traveled, and to question her personal motivations. As she continued her political work after 1967, she drew from these experiences in North Vietnam and linked the struggles of oppressed peoples worldwide—be they white, black, male, female, American, or Vietnamese. While her methods and ideology were constantly changing, she stayed true to her instincts and to a fundamental belief in human rights for all. Carol McEldowney's journal stands today, therefore, not only as the written record of an extraordinary trip in a tumultuous time, but also as a testament to the limitless potential of a human being who was willing to take unimaginable risks for the sake of better understanding the world in which she lived.

Notes

1. For examples of activists' writings on their trips to North Vietnam, see Daniel Berrigan, *Night Flight to Hanoi: War Diary with Eleven Poems* (1968); Elaine Brown, *A Taste of Power: A Black Woman's Story* (1992); David Dellinger,

From Yale to Jail (1993); Jane Fonda, *My Life So Far* (2005); Tom Hayden, *Reunion: A Memoir* (1989); Staughton Lynd and Tom Hayden, *The Other Side* (1966); Mary McCarthy, *Hanoi* (1969); Susan Sontag, *Trip to Hanoi* (1969); Ethel Barol Taylor, *We Made a Difference: My Personal Journey with Women Strike for Peace* (1998); and Howard Zinn, *You Can't Be Neutral on a Moving Train* (1994).

2. Carol McEldowney, untitled and undated essay, Papers of Carol McEldowney, Miscellaneous Papers, 1969–1973, 41, Joseph P. Healey Library, University of Massachusetts, Boston. Hereafter McEldowney Papers, Healey Library.

3. Lucille Cohen, tape-recorded interview with Suzanne K. McCormack, November 10, 2001; Gilbert Cohen, tape-recorded interview with Suzanne K. McCormack, November 10, 2001; Carol Vogt, telephone interview with Suzanne K. McCormack, December 3, 2001.

4. Lucille Cohen, November 10, 2001.

5. Wini Breines, "'Of This Generation': The New Left and the Student Movement," in *Long Time Gone: Sixties America Then and Now*, ed. Alexander Bloom (New York: Oxford University Press, 2001), 24.

6. James Miller, *"Democracy is in the Streets": From Port Huron to the Siege of Chicago* (New York: Simon & Schuster, 1987), 26.

7. Harlan Hatcher, "President's Welcome," *Michigan Daily* (Ann Arbor, Michigan), microfilm, September 13, 1960, 1.

8. Thomas Hayden, "The American Student," *Michigan Daily*, September 21, 1960, 4.

9. Ruth Evenhuis, "Voice Announces Platform Provisions," *Michigan Daily*, October 14, 1960, 2; VOICE, "Platform," adopted September 30, 1963, Papers of Students for a Democratic Society, microfilm, reel 7/2A. Hereafter SDS Papers.

10. VOICE, "Platform," 4.

11. U.S. Department of Justice, Federal Bureau of Investigation File no. 105-174411, Subject: Carol Cohen McEldowney, undated report including "Arrest Record," 5.

12. Deborah Cowles to Mr. and Mrs. Al Cohen, May 9, 1961, McEldowney Papers, Healey Library, 2.

13. Lucille Cohen, November 10, 2001.

14. "What is the S.D.S.?" undated pamphlet [before June 1962], SDS Papers, reel 1/1, 2.

15. Ibid., 1.

16. Ibid., 3.

17. Registration List, SDS Convention, June 11–15, 1962, SDS Papers, reel 1/1, 1–2.

18. Miller, *"Democracy is in the Streets,"* 329. The Port Huron Statement is reprinted in full as an appendix to Miller's book.

19. Ibid., 330.

20. Kirkpatrick Sale, *SDS* (New York: Random House, 1973), 663.

21. Carol McEldowney to "Marlene and Charlotte and all," July 1969, Carol McEldowney Papers, 1964–1971 (SC 648), State Historical Society of Wisconsin, 2, hereafter McEldowney Papers, SHSW; Sale, *SDS*, 5.
22. Ken and Carol McEldowney, "VOICE Political Party: A Critical History," SDS Papers, reel 7/2A, 1.
23. Ibid., 2.
24. Quoted in Nicholas Lemann, *The Promised Land: The Great Black Migration and How It Changed America* (New York: Vintage Books, 1991), 144–45.
25. Taylor Branch, *Pillar of Fire: America in the King Years, 1963–1965* (New York: Simon & Schuster, 1998), 291.
26. Robert Dallek, *Flawed Giant: Lyndon Johnson and His Times, 1961–1973* (New York: Oxford University Press, 1998), 83.
27. "Resolution of the 1964 S.D.S. Convention on Its Community Organizing Program," undated, SDS Papers, reel 2/2A, 1.
28. ERAP Fall Program, Report to the National Council, undated, SDS Papers, roll 2/2A, 2.
29. Ollie Fein to Lee [Webb], January 18, 1964, SDS Papers, roll 14/2B, 1.
30. Carl Wittman, "Report on Visit to Cleveland, February 1–2, 1964," SDS Papers, roll 14/2B, 1–2.
31. Report from Cleveland Community Project, June 20–28, 1964, SDS Papers, roll 10/2B, 1.
32. Carol McEldowney to Ren [Davis], September 15, 1964, SDS Papers, roll 14/2B, 1.
33. Estimated Budget of Students for a Democratic Society, November 1964–June 1965, SDS Papers, reel 6/2A, 3.
34. Carol McEldowney to "Art," September 21, 1964, SDS Papers, reel 14/2B, 1.
35. Ibid., 11.
36. Carol McEldowney to "Art," October 15, 1966, McEldowney Papers, Healey Library, Welfare: April 1966–April 1967, 1.
37. Carol Cohen McEldowney will henceforth be referred to as "McEldowney."
38. "An Introduction: Cleveland Community Project, Summer 1966," undated, McEldowney Papers, SHSW.
39. Carol McEldowney to Cuyahoga County Welfare Department, July 8, 1966, McEldowney Papers, SHSW, 1–2.
40. For more on the race riots that plagued American cities during Lyndon Johnson's presidency, see Peter Rossi, ed., *Ghetto Revolts* (New Brunswick, N.J.: Transaction Books, 1973); and Barbara Ritchie, *The Riot Report* (New York: Viking Press, 1969).
41. "Demonstration: For More School Clothing," August 19, 1966, McEldowney Papers, SHSW, 1.
42. "September Is Almost Here," undated flyer, McEldowney Papers, SHSW, 1.
43. Louise Lind, "Protesting Moms 'Buy,' Don't Pay," *Plain Dealer*, (Cleveland) undated clipping [August 1966], McEldowney Papers, SHSW, 7.

44. Kathy Boudin, Sharon Jeffrey, Carol McEldowney, and Paul Potter, "Crisis in Cleveland," [April 1967], McEldowney Papers, SHSW, 2–3.

45. Carol McEldowney, "The Radical and the Welfare System," paper presented at Conference on Radicals in the Professions, July 14–16, 1967, 1, Labadie Collection, Special Collections Library, University of Michigan.

46. Ibid., 5.

47. Carol McEldowney to Todd and Paul, December 16, 1964, SDS/PREP, McEldowney Papers, Healey Library; Carol McEldowney to Todd, February 13, 1965, SDS/PREP, McEldowney Papers, Healey Library. The pamphlets and booklets that McEldowney gathered on Vietnam, both the war and the nation's history, are in McEldowney Papers, Healey Library.

48. Marilyn Young, *The Vietnam Wars: 1945–1990* (New York: Harper Perennial, 1991), 334.

49. Ibid., 22.

50. George Herring, *America's Longest War: The United States and Vietnam, 1950–1975* (New York: McGraw Hill, 1996), 11.

51. Ibid., 43.

52. Ibid., 43.

53. Young, *The Vietnam Wars,* 333.

54. Herring, *America's Longest War,* 105–8.

55. Dallek, *Flawed Giant,* 17.

56. Young, *The Vietnam Wars,* 333.

57. Ibid., 333.

58. SDS pamphlet, "A Call to All Students to March on Washington to End the War in Vietnam," undated [before April 17, 1965], SDS Papers, reel 6, 1.

59. Charles DeBenedetti and Charles Chatfield, *An American Ordeal: The Antiwar Movement of the Vietnam Era* (Syracuse: Syracuse University Press, 1990), 111–12.

60. Carol McEldowney, "Summary of Discussion about Cleveland Community Project," May 1965, McEldowney Papers, Healey Library.

61. Sharon Jeffrey, "Vietnam in Poor Black and White Communities," *ERAP Newsletter,* August 14, 1965, SDS Papers, reel 11/2B, 12–13.

62. Ibid., 14.

63. Tom Wells, *The War Within: America's Battle over Vietnam* (New York: Henry Holt & Company, 1994), 584.

64. Christopher Jencks, "Negotiations Now? Reflections on a Meeting with the Enemy," *New Republic* 157, (October 7, 1967): 19–20.

65. Steve Halliwell, "A Society in Revolution," *New Left Notes,* October 2, 1967, 1.

66. John Pairman Brown, "A Visit to North Vietnam," *Christianity* 85 (January 3, 1968): 18.

67. Mary Hershberger, *Traveling to Vietnam: American Peace Activists and the War* (Syracuse: Syracuse University Press, 1998), xv–xvii.

68. Carol McEldowney, Journal of Trip to Hanoi, North Vietnam, September 21, 1967, 15. Hereafter cited only by date and page. Page numbers refer to the original manuscript.
69. September 21, 1967, 16.
70. September 26, 1967, 27–28.
71. September 30, 1967, 37–38.
72. Ibid., 40–41.
73. Ibid., 51.
74. October 1, 1967, 64.
75. Ibid.
76. October 2, 1967, 73.
77. October 3, 1967, 77.
78. Ibid., 78.
79. October 5, 1967, 102–3.
80. Ibid., 104.
81. October 6, 1967, 108.
82. Ibid., 110–11.
83. October 9, 1967, 131–35.
84. Ibid., 138.
85. October 11, 1967, 157–58.
86. Ibid., 158.
87. In addition to memoirs by individual prisoners, there are numerous published works on American POWs during the Vietnam War era, see Craig Howes, *Voices of the Vietnam POWs: Witnesses to Their Fight* (1993) and John G. Hubbell, *POW: A Definitive History of the American Prisoner-of-War Experience in Vietnam, 1964–1973* (1976). Tom Hayden's memoir *Reunion* (1988) also describes this particular meeting.
88. Hanoi Journal, 12 October 12, 1967, 157–58.
89. Ibid., 168,
90. Ibid., 169-70.
91. Ibid., 172.
92. Ibid., 172–73.
93. Ibid., 172–75.
94. October 17, 1967, 198.
95. Ibid., 199.
96. Ibid., 200–201.
97. October 18, 1967, 208–9.
98. October 19–20, 1967, 210–11.
99. October 25, 1967, 213.
100. Ibid., 218.
101. October 30, 1967, 226.
102. Ibid., 226–27.
103. October 31, 1967, 235.

104. Andrew Kopkind, "The Sixties and the Movement," *Ramparts* 11 (February 1973): 31.
105. Ibid., 33.
106. Carol McEldowney, untitled and undated essay, Miscellaneous Papers: 1969–73, McEldowney Papers, Healey Library, 37. McEldowney wrote this entire document in lower case letters seemingly for emphasis.
107. Carol McEldowney, "I Visited North Vietnam," *Plain Dealer Sunday Magazine,* (Cleveland), February 18, 1968, 58 and 61.
108. Carol McEldowney to Dickie Magidoff, September 15, 1968, in folder "Summary of discussion about Cleveland Community Project" by Carol Cohen McEldowney, May 1965–January 1969, McEldowney Papers, Healey Library, 2.
109. Carol McEldowney to "Norm, and Robert if you are there," November 19, 1967, in ibid., 2–3.
110. See letters on these and other topics of concern in ibid.
111. Carol McEldowney, "A Personal Manifesto . . . of sorts . . . thoughts about the movement," March 30, 1969, "Personal Manifesto, 1969–1971, part 1 of 4," McEldowney Papers, Healey Library, 2.
112. Carol McEldowney to "Carole and Sylvia, and whoever else," December 12, 1969, ibid., 70.
113. Carol McEldowney, untitled essay, April 10, 1971, "The Coming Out Journal, 1971–1973 , part 1 of 3," McEldowney Papers, Healey Library, 8.
114. McEldowney, untitled and undated essay, Miscellaneous Papers: 1969–73, 37.
115. Carol McEldowney, July 13, 1973, "Final Journal: June 1973–September 1973," personal collection of Katherine Roberts.

Hanoi Journal, 1967

European Preparations and the Journey to Hanoi, September 9–29, 1967

TRIP TO HANOI
September 1967

9 September 1967, I think, was the date we learned about the Hanoi trip. By the evening of the 11th selections were formalized, and the following people were to go[1]:

Tom Hayden
Vivian Rothstein
Rennie Davis
John Brown
John Wilson
Myself
Bob Allen (<u>National Guardian</u>)
Norm Fruchter
Ron Young
Stoney Cooks

The morning of the 13th everyone left for Prague, from Bratislava.[2] Nick Egleson[3] and some of the other Americans from the conference came to

---

[1] See introduction for the actual delegation.

[2] See introduction for description of Bratislava Conference.

[3] Nick Egleson was president of Students for a Democratic Society (SDS) during 1966–67. Kirkpatrick Sale, *SDS* (New York: Random House, 1973), 664.

3

Prague as well. I went to Vienna for a day to arrange airline tickets and the like.

13 September 1967—evening

In a Vienna hotel room—a strange one!—Carol Brightman (editor of Viet Report and a very sharp gal who spent a month in Hanoi last January for the war crimes tribunal),[4] spent hours talking.

She made many useful suggestions for the trip:

Places to visit:
1. Catholic provinces: main → Thanh Hoa, and Ninh Binh, Thai Binh, Nam Ha districts: Tinh Gia (in Thanh Hoa)
2. north of Hanoi: Viet-tri, Thai Nguyen, Phu Tho
3. northeast: Haiphong, Ha-long Bay, Hangai (a coal-mining region, resorts, and model worker's towns)
4. south: Ninh Binh and Thanh Hoa provinces
5. near Hanoi: Thai Binh (heavily populated and large rice producer)
6. working quarters near Long Bien Bridge, Hanoi

People:
1. Pham Ngoc Thach: Minister of Health
2. Dr. Lan Le Duan: head of mobile surgery team in Thanh Hoa (city area)
3. Dr. Pham Quy: head medical officer of Thanh Hoa province
4. Nguyen Van Vy: interpreter

Other suggestions:
1. ask regularly for: Associated Press (AP) and United Press International (UPI) releases,
2. propaganda: look for leaflets, transistor radios, etc. dropped along coast, all psychological warfare,
3. get pieces of (guava) bombs,
4. in villages, especially look at places where women hold administrative positions

---

[4] Refers to the War Crimes Tribunal held by the Bertram Russell Peace Foundation in Sweden in May 1967. The tribunal accused the U.S. government of atrocities in the conflict in Vietnam. John Duffett, ed., *Against the Crime of Silence: Proceedings of the Russell International War Crimes Tribunal* (New York: O'Hare Books, 1968), 3–5.

17 September 1967

Discussion with Ivo Vasiljev, Czech specialist and interpreter of Vietnamese—a warm, lovely man with a very deep feeling for the Vietnamese. Several suggestions of things to look for:
1. the English school, i.e., where English is taught,
2. phenomenon of towns with only women and children,
3. road-building brigades

We talked a lot about customs, a conversation continued September 20th with Pham Van Chuong of the NLF [National Liberation Front][5] mission in Prague. Many helpful suggestions. Ivo's main points were:
1. always smile,
2. respect local customs (dress, walking people outside, accepting food),
3. bring gifts,
4. inquire about behavior

Chuong added some:
1. greet each other by handshakes,
2. ask guides about photographing,
3. ask mothers about holding children

The general point of all: American and European customs are rather barbaric compared to a great deal of Vietnamese culture. Their culture is important to them, and disrespect for its importance is insulting. Discussing this dramatized for me how varied and untraditional our American culture is, and how unable we are to perform properly with foreigners. Part of it is a healthy dislike of fetish and a suspicion of formalities that lack sincerity. But the difference of the Vietnamese culture, according to Ivo and to many Vietnamese we have met, is that it is dear to them, an important element of their life, and part of their history that lives strong.

---

[5] Established in December 1960, the National Liberation Front (NLF) was a communist-led guerrilla group that sought to organize the countryside against the corruption of Diem's American-backed regime in Saigon. The organization, according to historian George Herring, was "designed to rally all those disaffected with Diem by promising sweeping reforms and establishment of genuine independence." George Herring, *America's Longest War: the United States and Vietnam, 1950–1975* (New York: McGraw-Hill, 1996), 74.

With Chuong we also compiled a brief list of common Vietnamese words and pronunciations: hello, good-bye, peace, independence. And we recorded these on the tape recorder. Chuong, it appeared, greatly enjoyed doing this—again that fierce pride of his country, which appears often and is accentuated by his hatred of being away and being forced to act as a "pseudo-diplomat" (his phrase), came out (more gently) as he taught us some of his language. For one heart-rending moment, he also referred to his wife, whom he recently married, and probably will not see for many months.

My own emotional reaction to this discussion with Chuong was very difficult (after pleasant, chatty dinner all together). When he left the hotel where we were staying, I had the distinct feeling I would not see him again, or any of the others we've met. I was struck hard with the realization of the many different levels of response to several people in particular. There is, of course, the political identity—and as an American, after all, Chuong and others must be hard-nosed about who I am and what I can do—or cannot. And the mere fact of the conference and the soon-to-be trip to Hanoi confirms the political alliance (more unquestionably for me, of course). But there is also the very personal emotional response to individuals, so human, so individual, and representing so many of the ideas and attitudes and qualities we cherish. Hardest, perhaps, is the romantic feeling: the Vietnamese are revolutionaries and something about that reaches in and touches the most romantic string in me—that feeling that makes me wish to be Vietnamese (and, at other times, black), and to no longer see that in front of my eyes, to not again see people with whom understandings, spiritual and political—have been reached, or at least approached, feels hard.

Preparation for trip: 17 September 1967ff.

Through a series of discussions together (Tom, Vivian, Stoney, Rennie, Jock, and myself, and Nick until he left Prague) we developed a list of key questions about the North, some to study beforehand, others to study there.

1. DRV [Democratic Republic of Vietnam][6]–NLF relationships. Negotiations: initiative came from DRV or NLF? Position of both DRV and NLF on this.

---

[6] Ho Chi Minh, as the leader of the Viet Minh, declared Vietnam's independence as the Democratic Republic of Vietnam in September 1945.

2. DRV government structure:
   - "how democracy works"—decentralization
   - internal division within DRV— organizationally
   - role of Communist Party—cell structure, etc.
   - internal conflicts: Catholic (anti-Ho) uprisings in north; massacre of Trotskyites[7]
3. Brief history and geography of DRV
4. Military situation
   - history of air war
   - terminology
   - preparation for war: understanding how in every phase of life people are mobilized for victory
     <u>how</u> is population politically mobilized?
     how are resources (agricultural and technological) used and new processes developed?
     how are systems of health and education applied?
5. Economy and the military:
   systems, techniques, methods of organization used and developed to fight the war—while building socialism: dikes, roads and communication, agricultural advances (new planting system)
6. International relations:
   - with Laos, Cambodia, Thailand
   - within the Chinese-Soviet sphere

Some other specific questions, more delicate, interest us all:
1. nature of Chinese and Soviet men and supplies to DRV
2. extent of DRV troops (non-regrouped) in South

There are also questions of our own attitudes and our own work after the trip. Specifically, while in Hanoi, can we prepare psychologically for the fact that we'll be under the bombs of the United States? Responses to this range from deadly serious to nervous giggles. Carol Brightman, when

---

[7] According to *The Pentagon Papers,* the Trotskyites were a revolutionary organization based in Saigon "who advocated anti-imperialist revolution throughout the world, and within Vietnam, expropriation for the workers and peasants." See the Senator Gravel edition of *The Pentagon Papers: The Defense Department History of the United States Decisionmaking on Vietnam,* vol. 1 (Boston: Beacon Press, 1971), 43.

she was in Hanoi, January 1967, had the experience of walking over a still-smoldering field. We were taken by the Czech Peace Committee to see Lidice, the town destroyed (razed) by the Nazis as a warning, its population massacred or put into concentration camps.[8] It is now a museum, with many graveyards—somber and evocative—on a grassy plot, hilly, a short walk from the new town. As we walked through and around the various historical markers, I could only anticipate, 10 days hence, walking much less casually, with a protection helmet, under bombs, in Hanoi. It is difficult to imagine, and now I cannot think of how I will describe it in several weeks.

We all are also likely to meet with American prisoners—pilots—and that may be a difficult experience, especially for Vivian, Jock, and me. But the worry about that has diminished. I question the political usefulness of that—but the humanity involved in doing it is essential, I think.

And, then, all the many questions of what to do when we get home. Some specifics:
1. how to assign tasks to the many dispersed people we will be.
2. establishing a decent communication system.
3. the war crimes tribunal: what should the American committee be? This is an area most of us know little about, to begin with.
4. U.S. peace movement. (We should prepare ourselves on the politics involved here, especially since the April mobilization.[9]) But what is our relationship to all this to be?

17 September 1967. Discussion with Ivo Vasiljev

We met at Ivo's home to begin discussion of some of the many questions we listed.

Ivo described the uniqueness of Vietnamese history: there, a unified political force existed prior to foreign occupation, in contrast to Germany and Korea where new political forces developed to correspond to territorial divisions. In spite of the war, NLF believes there is "normal intercourse" be-

---

[8] This occurred on June 10, 1942.

[9] McEldowney is referring to the April 15, 1967, Spring Mobilization to End the War in Vietnam, an event during which thousands of activists around the country took to city streets to protest the war. In San Francisco alone, more than fifty thousand protestors participated. Charles DeBenedetti, *An American Ordeal* (Syracuse: Syracuse University Press, 1990), 175.

tween north and south since 1962. NLF now has "international relations" with the DRV, which is the beginning of reunification.

DRV troops in the south? There are regrouped troops who went north after 1954 who have returned home. Those in the DRV are still under NLF jurisdiction. NLF open acknowledgement of the presence of troops would lead to U.S. justifying further escalation and eliminating any distinction between fighting the war in the north and south. In addition, NLF wants to keep clear the U.S. violation of Geneva Agreements.

(This becomes one of those matters where even anti-war Americans become brainwashed about the questions we ask. Given the nature of the war, the presence of DRV troops in the south is irrelevant. If we ask this for making military assessments of strength, that is one thing. But the very question implies a judgment about such troops.)

Ivo also described some of his reactions to the NLF delegation at Bratislava. At least 3 people are key high-up's who attended the NLF Congress. They are Madame Binh (head of the Delegation at Bratislava and Vice-President of Liberation Women's Union[10] and probably a member of the NLF Central Committee?); Dinh Ba Thi, NLF Ambassador to Budapest; and Ha Thanh Lam, the Buddhist layman who recently became the NLF ambassador to Prague, which is a crucial mission because of contact with West. (Lam's appointment probably suggests his very high importance now). Nguyen Van Hieu, a journalist from the south, was formerly the number one agent in Prague (he is on the NLF Central Committee and is National Secretary of the PRP (?), and is now ambassador to Phnom Penh).

Communist Party: DRV and South Vietnam parties have been and are quite separate. In the South insurrections as early as 1940 were opposed by the North. North's opposition to Southern insurrections (which were started by non-Communists and only joined later) extended into 1950's; there was fear of East-West relations being affected by Southern revolt.

---

[10] The Viet Nam Women's Union, the first Vietnamese women's organization, was formed in 1930 and linked to the Indochinese Communist Party (ICP). According to Arlene Eisen Bergman, the women supported the work of the ICP, which advocated an end to French rule in Vietnam and generous access to land for peasants. The women, according to Bergman, "worked to include all working women in their organization and others who were not part of the constituency of the trade union and peasant organizations. In 1930, heavy French repression forced the Women's Union to be a clandestine organization." Arlene Eisen Bergman, *Women of Viet Nam* (San Francisco: People's Press, 1974), 50–52.

During the French resistance, there were 4 sections of the CP: north, became Lao Dong; pan-handle area; Hue and south; southern peninsula.

On May 1, 1958, a national unified front was established as a movement. This preceded by 2 years the Front as an organization. There were early splits, but the DRV was forced to support the Front. Reactions to southern insurrections of 1958 were varied: the DRV tried to establish relations with Diem as late as December 1958, final communication was after the Phom Lai massacre.[11] The Russians feared the implications for coexistence. The Chinese said they were not prepared to defend South Vietnam, but in June 1958 Mao Tse Tung said Chinese bombs would exist in 10 years.

By 1959 the Southern Communists had joined the Front. And the 1959 Congress of the Lao Dong[12] referred to political goals for both the North and the South.

21–23 September 1967

Reflections on coming trip:

I have thought long and hard about the reasons for going to Hanoi, yet I have not thought at all. . . . In Bratislava, the opportunity to go seemed the once-in-a-lifetime chance. I was convinced by the arguments of the personal effect it would have on me, the need to develop a long-range perspective on the (peace) movement, the need for community organization work to have more contact with and affect the anti-war movement. And naturally I was affected by Nick and Tom saying it would be an invaluable experience . . . etc. Of course, the fact that the possibility arose while in the middle of a meeting with the Vietnamese whetted my desire to not only hear but to see.

I have and have had many reservations—many confusing thoughts and questions:
- what is my political reason for going?
- are "personal interest" reasons enough justification?
- money, obligations in Cleveland?
- should a non-writer, non-speaker, non–peace movement activist go? Is that indulgence?
- responsibilities after the trip? How to decide them sensibly?
- and others . . .

---

[11] Ngo Dinh Diem was prime minister and president of South Vietnam from 1954 to 1963.

[12] The Vietnamese Workers Party.

In Bratislava, I was able to answer some of these questions in a partly satisfying manner.

1. There is a great need for Americans to know and understand the war, the bombing, and the society of the DRV. Conversations at the conference were a beginning. But there is no doubt that actually seeing the war and meeting the Vietnamese in their own land will teach a lot more. (I thought the people at the conference who were not interested in going to Hanoi because "I've learned all I need to know—or enough—from this conference to help me in my work" were superficial or naïve in thinking or believing they had learned enough.)

   This is personally valuable and valuable for the movement, as well, to have more and more people who have had direct contact with the DRV.

2. I agreed on the importance of community organizers seeing the war and feeling a new and deeper responsibility for bringing our movement and the peace movement closer together. For too long we've not taken enough responsibility in thinking with the anti-war movement.

3. Aside from the strong desire to go to the DRV, my availability afterwards and lack of any unalterable commitments made me want to go—the same feelings that propelled me towards Bratislava to begin with. The feeling of uncertainty about what to do next (whither welfare organizing, etc.?), a searching, a willingness to be affected . . . all these made me feel it was good to go. But all this also greatly tempered by a variety of other feelings: I have been critical of many anti-war activities, because they lack a political perspective and do not lead to building permanent organized bases. Knowing that I am being "turned on," I don't want to lose my head and go off on some cockeyed peacenik scheme. For me it is important to maintain contact with whatever cadre develops out of the conference, to be a critical political judge of strategy and planned projects. And I don't want to be swept away by the intrigue of underground organization or whatever without a great deal of careful thought.

Further thoughts:

No doubt that I (all of us) have been "turned on" by this experience. But I feel confident of already being a confirmed radical, and I don't think the trip to Hanoi is needed to establish my commitment.

Vivian and I have talked a lot over all these questions, and we share many similar misgivings. She (and Rennie, too) are even more troubled than I because they have firm commitments to a certain organizing project(s) which is not necessarily going to be anti-war.

What are the political reasons for going? Frankly I'm not sure. (I could be more certain if I knew I would write or speak publicly. I will try both but neither is my forté.) I do believe it is important for American radicals to have a long range and sensitive perspective of American foreign policy. Vietnam is the ugliest example, but U.S. imperialism will continue when Vietnam has peace. And as long as we are going to work to change America, we must be more aware of the rest of the world and where the U.S. fits.

There is no doubt about the personal effect the trip will have on me. It will be vastly educational. It may help me think of new forms of organizing. It will make me a valuable resource for the movement in the U.S. (good for me and the movement!). And for once, I feel like the absence of clear-cut political reasons for going is <u>not</u> a reason to <u>not go</u>. The untold potential values of going are too great to risk losing.

Some specific thoughts of things to do afterwards:
1. Vivian and I both can work with women. Should we try to influence WSP [Women Strike for Peace], organize local chapters, etc.?[13] We are both so struck by the role of the Vietnamese women in the liberation struggle and for women's independence. Can we reach American women with that message and mobilize them?
   * What are the constituencies to which we have particular access by virtue of being women, of being fresh faces on the anti-war front?
2. We (I) could organize more conferences like Bratislava. We will now be among the privileged few with direct contacts, and could play an important role (part-time) in expanding contact of Americans with Vietnamese.
3. Could make ourselves available to SDS [Students for a Democratic Society] regions to establish contacts with students—speaking, informal gatherings.
4. Most important, probably, is to try to influence the thinking and the direction of the peace movement in our respective locales. Also the most difficult since it requires thinking through, more clearly than I

---

[13] WSP was an antiwar and anti-nuclear organization formed in 1961 by white, middle-class housewives concerned for their children's future.

yet have, such a perspective. Someone, I think, must maintain the basic job of "international agent" and Tom of course is the likely choice. Most of us should, I believe, continue base-building work with the value of our newly acquired views on the war and the peace movement. More later on that . . . "internationalism and the movement."

5. Specifically, I am interested in doing some propaganda work. Some related to organizing GI's (very hazy on this, except perhaps tapes for the NLF); the whole task of keeping Chuong and others informed, which might put me into an "information-gathering" job for awhile. I am interested in perhaps doing a filmstrip on the DRV—if we can plan it well and in advance. And when I return, I am open to full-time work for several months as post-conference work—if a group can be brought together (however informally) to provide some guidance.

23rd September 1967. Scattered reflections on Prague en route to Phnom Penh

Two and one-half weeks in Czechoslovakia—a week in Bratislava and the rest in Prague. Impressions of the country are very scattered and unorganized. In Bratislava I didn't go into the town as other Americans did frequently. Their experience gave them the impression of dissatisfied youth: pro-Western, pro-Israel, anti-Cuba, and anti-government, though the many reasons are hard to decipher. In Prague our impressions came from several different individuals or groups. We had to spend an ungodly amount of time in preparations (visas for Cambodia, hotel accommodations, Czech visas extended, eating, cholera shots) and much of that time was spent with the Czech Peace Committee, particularly one man fairly new to the scene. They were generous people, interested in us, but very much party men. An entirely different view was expressed through Anna, a 23-year-old girl who speaks English and who was employed in the college dormitory we stayed in the first 3 nights. She is trying to go to England for 6 months to study the language, and she became our personal guide for the week we were there: everything from exchanging money at black market rates to taking me shopping to showing us food places to doing Tom and Rennie's laundry. The line of exploitation was not clear. Often I felt we were taking advantage of her (enormously), but on the other hand she was getting a lot of American dollars from us which she needs to travel, and a chance to practice

English. (My own feelings inclined towards the former and, admittedly, I was biased by the men's attitudes. . . .) But in any case, she spoke rather freely and critically of the government and common attitudes shared by the youth. Most substantively, she believes the government is a dictatorship by workers which discriminates against intellectuals and other non-workers. The police are repressive—there is not enough freedom of speech, and subtle (or not-so-subtle) forms of discrimination are used against dissenters (e.g., kicking students out of school). She also complained of the rising costs of living, the undependable services, the difficulty in traveling to western countries. Throughout all this was an absolute resignation and very little hope. The Party, she claimed, was inflexible: some of her friends had joined it to try to change it. Either they were changed themselves or they quit. Yet she plans to return to Czechoslovakia from England. Interesting, also, that she doesn't look to the west for "models"—Yugoslavia, she said, was the country admired by many of her friends. And China she feared. Who knows how much to generalize from her attitudes to the country's youth?

What was abundantly clear, however, is the presence of a generational conflict. As interesting as the Peace Committee people were, and even Ivo (who, because of his love for the Vietnamese, is much more gentle and less bureaucratic a person), they all took strict Party lines dogmatically and inflexibly when we spoke of youth dissent, changing societies, etc. (Naturally concerned and puzzled about the role of the CP in the American movement.) The last night in Prague we all drank famous black beer together at U Flěcku,[14] and everyone loosened up. Vivian and I then had a conversation with Sechousky where he really took off against the irresponsible youth, in hackneyed language—it was a sad scene. Partly, of course, language poses a difficult problem. But we were very struck by the feeling that we were getting the official line—most dramatically when we spoke of the youth, but also when we tried to critically raise questions about the economy, social organizations, etc.

Other scattered impressions of Prague range from the lucrative black market; to a discussion I had with Kathy [Boudin]'s friend Joseph Cort (American living in Prague 13 years) and Vladimir, mostly about the movement in the U.S.—a little bit of party line from Vladimir, too; an afternoon journey to Lidice (town razed by the Nazis as an "example" which made me think much more of how I would feel under American bombs in Hanoi); walking around the city a lot—beautiful, historically rich city, but very gray

---

[14] A tavern in Prague.

and drab in many ways; heavy Czech food; free medicine and truly social-ized medicine which I experienced twice—first having a sore finger, and later needing a cholera shot for Cambodia.

22 September: Day spent with Tran Van An.

Met at NLF, talked a while about my coming Hanoi trip. He warned me of the dangers of going to Saigon. Went to I.U.S. [International Union of Students], met Vok, talked about "Week of Solidarity," Nov. 11–17th. Lunch together at Peking Restaurant—learned to use chopsticks. Long walk back to Peace Committee. Lovely day. Sad farewell.

Sunday, 24th September 1967: Phnom Penh

Quick reactions to the long journey—now waiting for Hanoi. Plane left Prague (late) 10 a.m. Saturday—old Russian bomber converted into pas-senger plane—amidst many farewells and a send-off by the Peace Commit-tee, Anna, Ivo Vasiljev, and Pham Van Chuong.

Stops:
1. Beirut: awful, awful. Airport is tourist trap. The men grab the women, and they all hate Americans. Horrible feeling to sit trapped in the transit lounge. The city looks beautiful—mountains, and the beautiful Mediter-ranean, which was magnificent to fly over. Exquisitely blue, and the coast-line of Turkey and Cyprus was delicately outlined the whole way under a perfectly clear sky.

From Beirut we flew over the Saudi Arabia desert—another indescrib-able view: endless miles of craters, red soil (Israel off to one side, Damascus visible from the air), then so high that it looked like red dust below us.

2. In the middle evening we made a brief stop at Dubai (wherever that is). It was sickeningly Americanized: a tiny tourist transit lounge with a small showcase of American products in the middle (perfume, jewelry, and toys). My sole memory will be of a little Arab man (in native clothes) displaying a toy U.S. Army tanker which played patriotic tunes when wound up. Really unnerving.

On the plane 2 Russian girls asked me to join them. They are teachers returning from Moscow for the last of 2 years of teaching near Phnom Penh. Some interesting conversations about my coming trip and our respective work. Mostly nice and social. And difficult to communicate in pidgin English and French.

3. Bombay—late at night—with an excellent free meal served in the airport. Very Indian. Very different.

4. Early a.m.—Rangoon—and for the first time I knew we were in the Orient. The absolutely lush green fields, the bamboo huts, the irrigation system visible from the air, the music in the airport (and the people)—suddenly realized how close we were to Hanoi and that we were in a completely different part of the world.

5. Phnom Penh. Arrived on time. A new day (the time changes are thoroughly disorienting).

To be continued . . .

26th September 1967

. . . Waiting to leave for airport to meet others of American delegation (2–4 of them). Have been in this city 2 days now. What hits one first is the heat—dramatically. A sticky, sultry sun which drives white people indoors though the people of the city go on through the heat of the day. The strange variety of odors hits second: much fish, and much that is unfamiliar. It pervades as you walk around, and for the first day the combination of sun and smell created faintness. (By the 2nd day I was adjusting.) Finally (and of course most significant in the long run) is the culture which I am not yet sure how to characterize. In the hotel: many Cambodian boys bowing at your service, almost tripping over you; hundreds of taxi drivers (cycles) waiting to pounce; very dramatic influence of the French from the restaurants to some clothing to little boys peddling books and cigarettes and knowing some of the language; to, of course, the entire effect of the Royaume du Cambodge;[15] miserable poverty, and a surprising degree of class difference; streets lined with Chinese, Vietnamese, and Cambodian shops, many of which also house total families who can be seen eating and sleeping on their floors (many of the stores have names tri-lingually: Cambodian, Chinese or Vietnamese, and French). The presence of colonialism and imperialism:

---

[15] Kingdom of Cambodia.

French mansions, Shell and Esso gasoline; and a small but dramatic example of a small carrying bag I bought which was lined at the bottom for support with a flattened Coke tin.

Americans are rare here, though apparently it is not that difficult to get visas. But who knows how we are seen? The country is an enigma politically. Colonized by the French and granted its independence under the Geneva Agreements, it is run by the prince whose position is hereditary and elective. Its role in southeast Asian affairs is a puzzle: they recognize the NLF, outlaw the Communist Party, no longer have relations with the U.S. (broken several years ago when it became clear the U.S. was bombing Cambodian villages on the South Vietnamese border), and just recently has been eliminating pro-Maoist forces within the Prince's cabinet and reducing relations with Peking.

Who are the agents here? Can one tell? A young, attractive Cambodian who speaks English fluently (schooled in the U.S. for 3 years) helped us at the airport—seemed to expect us and knew where we were going. Later appeared at our hotel, offered more help, but rather mysteriously (though smilingly) only identified himself as someone employed by the airport and a travel agency. Hard to believe. But whose payroll is he on?

Late evening: awful experience. Vivian and I went with "sister" of Ivo and her boyfriend to "see the town." They took us to a cabaret-style club, with dancing girls and American music and motion. It was at least his idea of good entertainment. He was educated 4 years in the U.S. and is terribly cool. The influence of the west on him and this country is frightening. (Couldn't really tell what Ivo's sister Kim thought.)

Wednesday, 27th September 1967. Siem Reap[16]

We made it here, Vivian, Norm Fruchter, and I, this afternoon, for a quickie tour of Angkor Wat and then back to Phnom Penh and to Hanoi Friday. Drive here was about 300 kilometers—and the countryside was perfectly strange and amazing—rice, people, thatched huts, pagodas, palm trees, swamp-lands, irrigation systems, water buffalos, crowded market places. And more.

Tonight's experience was rare. After dinner we walked some and were drawn to Cambodian music. Wound up in front of an old barn-like hall and

---

[16] Provincial capital and old colonial town in Cambodia.

stood outside, wondering if it was proper to enter. Finally negotiated in pidgin French and got in to what turned out to be probably the best example of local village entertainment: amateur performance (quite clearly "lower class") of an inane fairy-tale story of good kings, bad villains, lovers, duels, mistaken identity, and the rest. Very slapstick. Very crude. Very long. But also very fascinating. Good view of Cambodian life.

Thursday, 28th September 1967. <u>Night before Hanoi</u>

A long set of complicated thoughts. First, some on students and internationalism, and the movement (especially resulting from Prague). Throughout the trip, my lack of knowledge of a foreign language has made me constantly aware of a certain provincialism of American students, especially as I've met political youth who know several languages. More than that, I've realized how little I personally (and probably many other movement people) know about the international student scene, in any substantive way. (I don't even know it in a skeleton fashion.)

One particular experience in Prague dramatized this. Tran Van An and I went together to the I.U.S. to discuss a planned week of "International Solidarity with Vietnamese Students" November 11th–17th. I was asked first about American student action, and then about what relations might, could, or do exist between American students and groups like I.U.S. I felt totally uninformed and answered honestly, cautiously, and not very helpfully. But, aside from my scanty knowledge of the membership of I.U.S., the formation of the ISC [International Student Conference], and the history of student groups in the Cold War, I didn't know if I was being totally naïve, being used, being laughed at, being helpful. I instinctively feel closer to the I.U.S. but am not sure if that is relevant. Is the I.U.S. relevant? What could be the significance of American groups working with it? How much contact does SDS have with international student groups (or foreign groups) and of what nature? I was struck suddenly by the realization that I could answer none of these questions, had no basis of knowledge or ideological framework for approaching them. And didn't know who to ask. . . .

In the specific situation, I primarily got information about the November 11th–17th week which I promised to communicate to American students via SDS. But in the longer run, I must think more about these questions, and their implication for the movement. I find it too easy to get carried away by the romanticism of internationalism, and have been a critic of programs in that direction because they don't build bases in the U.S. But it nevertheless seems timely to ask whether it's important now for SDS to develop more systematic ties with other student movements in the world. The question is useful, regardless of the answer. Norm Fruchter suggested that there are international ties growing, especially related to draft organizing, and that is something I should investigate further when I get home.

Also talked with Norm about follow-up to Bratislava conference and new job possibilities—similar discussion I've had with Kramer, Kopkind, Jencks.[17]

Had a very useful (and liberating-for-an-evening) conversation with Bob Allen. We talked about the role of white radicals in America now, given the presence of a black revolutionary force. Who should whites be organizing (poor people? workers? students? middle class? anyone and everyone?) and what are the self-interests of those groups (especially economic) that would ever make them supportive of the black movement? What contact should white radicals have and develop with 3rd world movements and what should be their base (I keep thinking of the importance of student organizing, but what thrust should it take: anti-draft, anti-imperialist?). What should all of us be doing in and to the present peace movement? And what would a radical peace movement be?

I can't help but return to the need for an organization of white radicals (or for us all to be reincorporated into, or equally appended to, SDS). This came up again in the conversation with Norm.

No answers to any of this yet, but I'm excited in thinking about it all, and (still tentatively) find it much easier to say I should exit from Glenville.[18]

Friday, 29 September 1967. Over North Vietnam

Reactions not yet sorted out. We are finally so close to being in Hanoi—leg 2 of the trip. So close it seems certain we will arrive, yet much too possible we won't. First part of the flight made me very sick; then we stopped in Vientiane, for a 3 hour wait. Airport was filled with various CIA [Central Intelligence Agency] and other American aircraft, used to bomb the Pathet

---

[17] Robert Kramer was an American film director, mainly of political films, including *In the Country* (1967); Andrew Kopkind was an editor of the *New Republic*; Christopher Jencks wrote for the *New Republic*.

[18] The neighborhood in Cleveland where McEldowney lived and worked for a time as part of the ERAP project (see introduction).

Lao.[19] We saw many such planes arrive and depart during our wait. The airport was not pleasant. We had the distinct feeling everyone there knew who we are, and probably don't like us any the better for it. The presence of the ICC [International Control Commission] [20] is not that comforting, either, although the English of the Indians and Canadians is a mild relief. We were treated to witnessing the ceremonial arrival of the Japanese Prime Minister Sato whose reception almost prevented our departure. Many Frenchmen at the airport, some Canadians, the complete mystery of the Laotian government. The plane is one of 2 of the ICC (the 3rd was lost), a private French plane labeled F-BELU, probably equivalent to a DC-4 in size, and it must fly, we have been informed, high and within a 30-foot-wide channel. We are flying over war. A Canadian ICC member claims a high percentage of planes are unable to land in Hanoi (due to weather—euphemistic for bombs?) and must return to Phnom Penh; in which case we cannot attempt take-off until Tuesday. Don't know how I feel about landing. I am excited but unable to record emotions and reactions beyond that. (Only hope it is not necessary to turn around.) We're all exhausted—it's soon to begin. We've prepared as comprehensive a list as possible of things we want to see and do in the DRV: priority to village life. Hopefully we can stay 2 weeks and cram things in. Next recording from Hanoi?

---

[19] The Pathet Lao were a communist-led Laotian independence movement supported by the Viet Minh. Marilyn Young, *The Vietnam Wars, 1945–1990* (New York: Harper Perennial, 1991), 38–41.

[20] Also called the International Commission for Supervision and Control, it was set up by the Geneva Conference in 1954 to supervise the cease-fire and reunification of Vietnam. The ICC consisted of Canada, India, and Poland, three countries not directly involved in the conflict. Marc Leepson, ed., *Webster's New World Dictionary of the Vietnam War* (New York: Webster's New World, 1999), 180–81.

Hanoi, September 29–October 17, 1967

Hanoi, Day 1: Friday, September 29.
Arrives in Hanoi

Friday September 29, 1967, Hanoi
Khách san Thống-nhất (Reunification Hotel)

Nous sommes arrivés!

From the air could see many lights over the city—I was surprised. Also the bridge over the Red River which was bombed while the DRV delegation was en route to Prague and still not completely repaired. Therefore we came to the city from the airport (where we were greatly welcomed, with flowers and much warmth) on a road (route 5) and then a ferry. A symbolic beginning. Strong pungent smell in the air; shelter holes along the road; ferry-repair crews; U.S. floodlights searching for planes (2 more American planes downed today, we were told); many helmets and what seemed to be a fair amount of traffic on the road, fairly easy trip, it turned out. To Reunification Hotel: fancy, large, very French. Dinner in our rooms tonight (Vivian and I together, guys on other floor), served by a perfectly impeccable man who undoubtedly served the French. Two huge beds with mosquito netting, much furniture in the rooms. Exhausted now, am sure I'll sleep at least tonight. So good to be met by friends. The conference in Bratislava was an invaluable first step for us. Breakfast at 7:30 a.m.—and discussion then of our plans, program, schedule.

Hanoi, Day 2: Saturday, September 30. Driving tour of the city; plan program for visit; Museum of the Vietnamese People's Army; evening banquet and documentary films

Saturday, Hanoi, 30th September 1967

Awoke early to the many noises outside—bells, bicycles, horns, but mostly the rain. It is an early city—like Phnom Penh. One important reason is the weather: to the extent that it affects bombing conditions, it is crucial. For example, the dangerous times to be outside in the city are 10 a.m. and 3–4 p.m.—at these times the sun is located in such a position that planes can fly into it more easily without being clear targets. During the day there are quick rain-showers.

After breakfast (a fine European meal) we took a drive around the city. The city shows much French influence—wide streets, large spacious-looking homes, tree-lined avenues. But the effects of the war are all over; beginning with the moment we step into our cars or walk outside, we carry our heavy (Russian-made?) helmets. The buildings are old and little has been done to maintain or upgrade physical condition, in anticipation of the worst. The city is very much evacuated. The absence of children is very noticeable. The large city market is no longer in use; the city is divided into various quarters for the purpose of providing food supplies. As we drove around, we saw other signs of war: manholes which serve as "abns" (shelters); many young girls in helmets; training units; victory signs (billboards) even inside the very peaceful pagoda we visited. That was our first stop, Chūa Môt Côt (One-Pillar Pagoda), 918 years old and headed by a 78-year-old bonze.[21] Built in the shape of a lotus flower, it was indeed a peaceful first stop, preparation, perhaps, for what was/is to follow . . . ?

We continued driving, passing the Presidential Palace, National Assembly building, and Independence Square; and our second stop (also peaceful) was Vuon Hoa Thong Nhat, Unity Park, signifying the cooperation of North-Central-South (Hanoi, Hue, Saigon) and constructed by the youth. Across the enlarged lake stands the evacuated Polytechnical Institute, built with Soviet aid.

As we drove back to the hotel, we passed the most recent Hanoi bombing, on Phō Hao, 22 August—workers' homes—purposeless bombing.

---

[21] A Buddhist monk.

In retrospect, at the end of the day, the drive around was probably one of the most serene experiences we will have.

Back at the hotel, Xuan Oanh[22] gave us the Peace Committee's proposed agenda for our stay:

Saturday, September 30th:
    afternoon: Museum of Vietnamese People's Army
    dinner: Vietnamese, with Peace Committee and people we met in
        Bratislava
    evening: new documentary films
Sunday, October 1st:
    6 a.m.: Museum of the Revolution
    afternoon: free
    6 p.m.: Catholic Mass for those interested (bomb damage)
    evening: cultural performance
Monday, October 2nd:
    whole day with Hanoi Committee for the Investigation of War Crimes
        (see damage in and near Hanoi).
Tuesday, October 3rd:
    whole day with Trade Union Organization: see factories, speak with
        workers, dinner also.
Wednesday, October 4th:
    see hospital in Hanoi, talk to victims, see weapons exhibition.
Thursday, October 5th:
    a.m.: see school on outskirts of Hanoi; women's school (3 Responsibili-
        ties),[23] meet militia women.
    afternoon: begin 3-day trip to countryside (place still undecided).
        There, see everything: bomb damage; production (cooperative
        farm); culture; public health; mobile surgery unit; education;
        fighting (militia, self-defense); family life; factory (including local
        administrative meeting, perhaps).
Till Sunday, October 8th:
    evening: meet with VPA [Vietnamese People's Army][24] to plan meeting
        captured pilots.

---

[22] Guide and translator for the delegation.

[23] McEldowney discusses the 3 Responsibilities later in her journal.

[24] North Vietnamese army.

Monday, October 9th:
   whole day with students and youth: see schools, get information on
      education, etc.
Tuesday, October 10th:
   meeting with ethnic minorities
   meetings with captured pilots.
Wednesday, October 11th:
   a.m.: see religious leaders
   afternoon: visit film studio
   evening: mass meeting of Vietnamese intellectuals to whom we will
      speak.
Thursday, October 12th:
   meeting with journalists
   visit night school
Friday, October 13th: Departure

Other things will be filled in, Wednesday and Thursday: meeting with officials, propaganda discussions (radio station), Hanoi culture—movies, athletics?

In addition, we can get news releases, as well as Voice of America and BBC on the radio.

Staff people include:
   Ha Huy Tâm—interpreter
   Nguyen Khoa Toan—guide (lives in Room 31 of hotel)
   Mr. Ly—Peace Committee bureaucrat, in charge of trip (?)
   (Dang Thai Toan—the guy who spoke no English but of the Peace Committee) and
   Xuan Oanh
   Nguyen Trung Hieu

Their agenda was planned (or adjusted) in response to a collective list we submitted. Most of our requests were included. We asked to see/do the following:
   1. Village—live in countryside several days. Other requests incorporated into province trip will be: see mobile surgery unit working in shelter; talk to students and teachers of evacuated schools; talk with workers

of cooperative and factory—administrative committees rarely meet due to war.

2. See recently bombed areas: Haiphong is unlikely since it is now the main target.

3. Speak with students learning English: the teachers' training courses are now located far from Hanoi—too difficult to travel.

4. Road-repair, dike brigades: this will probably be arranged through the youth.

5. Meet minority peoples: to be done through Institute of Minorities.

6. Entertainment troupe: the "cream of the artists" are far from Hanoi, near the 17th parallel, but some have been invited to return for an evening of song and dance. (It will be hard for us to arrange "spontaneous" culture, I fear.)

7. Speak with officials—Ministries of Public Health, Education: we will meet representatives when we see schools and hospitals.

8. Speak to major government officials, submit questions, and perhaps obtain taped message for the October 21st demonstration.[25] The 3 major officials are President Ho Chi Minh, Premier Pham Van Dong, Speaker of Parliament (National Assembly Chairman) Truong Chinh, proposed by Peace Committee (hasn't met with American group yet).

9. Discussion about propaganda: we will meet with Nguyen Minh Vy, Department of Information, about this.

10. Speak with captured pilots: no problem. Will be arranged by Defense Ministry. Important, according to Oanh, for all of us to "educate" them—they will want to see their fellow compatriots.

11. See filmmakers, studio (special request by Norm). Oanh stressed that the filmmakers would be glad to see all of us, a point he has made several times about the group going together.

12. Gather U.S. propaganda leaflets.

13. Make tapes for GIs, talk to Mr. Vy about both [12 and 13].

14. Collect bomb fragments—probably can be gathered at bombsites.

15. Evidence of B-52's that were downed: not officially reported yet by DRV standards, and not clear if the planes landed in the North or the South.

16. Revolutionary Museum in Hanoi: planned.

---

[25] McEldowney is referring to the antiwar march on the Pentagon on October 21, 1967. Between 50,000 and 100,000 protesters marched from a rally at the Lincoln Memorial to the Pentagon.

We were a little surprised at their desire to keep us together. But the practical problems of translation and travel security are more easily dealt with when we are in a group.

Other miscellaneous thoughts: everyone is going to be given a pair of Ho Chi Minh sandals. Our feet were measured. And we will be able to take back pairs for our respective men and women. In addition, Vivian, Jock,[26] and I are going to have special (traveling) trousers made, and Vivian and I are also getting black Vietnamese trousers. All with the compliments of the Peace Committee!

[The following section was a typed page inserted in the journal.]
Written before arriving in Hanoi: some thoughts on things I would like to do during the trip:

Most generally, I am interested in trying to understand the kind of society the DRV is building, under the pressure of war, and what clues are to be seen about what that society will look like in peacetime? Try to appreciate how the DRV has brought about decentralization, and mobilization of the population, and what have been the effects?

On decentralization:
- see decentralized and/or evacuated industry
- see schools, hospitals, etc., that have been moved out of Hanoi

On mobilization of the population:
- see women's self-defense units
- talk to road building, repairing brigades
- see role of local population in public health; how is preventive medicine organized?
- mobilization of the youth for military action

In general, on the nature of the society:
• See village life, in as many ways as possible:
- see changing agricultural patterns, introduction of new technology, effects
- life of women and changing family patterns, especially with the absence of men
- local health and educational facilities: how they are run, content
- administration of villages

---

[26] John Brown.

- youth: from their position where will the society be in peacetime? talk with Student Union, young women

Effect of bombing: try to see areas not yet visited by Americans; emphasis on bridges, roads, towns, working quarters.
Talk to prisoners.
Get propaganda, especially psychological warfare stuff, such as leaflets dropped by U.S. planes.

In Hanoi:
- see Museum of the Revolution
- talk with students at English (Language) Institute
- get some sense of cultural life in city (movies?)
- get daily AP and UPI wire releases

Specific people to talk to:
- Pham Ngoc Thach (suggested by Carol Brightman)
- Nguyen Van Huyen, or someone with national view on education system
- Dr. Lan Le Duan (mobile surgery unit in Thanh Hoa, if we get there)
- other officials: government and organization???

[End of inserted typed page.]

September 30, <u>more</u>

Afternoon discussions with John-Pierre Vigier, French military expert working with the War Crimes Tribunal. His remarks summarized:

Haiphong is being constantly bombed: ⅓ of the city is destroyed, another third is being bombed. There are 4 ways to destroy a harbor: naval blockade; destroy the coves; destroy the city; ground blockade. But regardless of the method used, the Americans will not be able to prevent the use of the coast—ships will still be able to disembark.

Intensive bombing began September 20th—all Seventh Fleet action. Night bombing is still on a small scale. There have been few losses, partly because the city is nearly empty, partly because people there are prepared.

Vo Nguyen Giap[27] has just written a significant new analysis of the war.

---

[27] General in the People's Army of Vietnam, influential in defeating the French at Dien Bien Phu.

He states 3 premises: the U.S. ambition is to conquer the world; the U.S. has been defeated in Vietnam; world resistance (à la Guevara[28]) must be organized to fight U.S. The U.S.'s next and only choice is to increase the air war—genocide, using special warfare. (Air war against China is not possible now.) On politics of the Tribunal: its job is to expose the war in Vietnam as an example of U.S. war against all 3rd world peoples. The war will be long, but the Vietnamese are "over the hump" and this pattern will be repeated everywhere.

1 October 1967—late

Saturday lunch: Oanh gradually opens up more. We have not learned what triggers him. We asked a number of questions to which he gave 1-sentence answers—then suddenly began to speak of families as the holiest unit in Vietnam, and then of evacuation. They try to evacuate children to villages where they already have relatives, because of traditional family closeness. Some families can make individual arrangements for transporting their children. Sometimes the children are moved by groups, for example, they will evacuate children of Peace Committee members together because it will facilitate visiting arrangements. On some occasions groups like the Students' or Women's Union will build (straw) villages for children who must be evacuated.

We find the statistics about evacuation difficult to believe. The city seems crowded, yet ⅔ of the nearly 1 million people who populated Hanoi and the outskirts have been evacuated. It is hard to imagine what the city would be like were those people here—where would they live?

Lunch was interrupted by our first air alert. We grabbed our helmets and retreated to the special guest shelter, while hotel staff donned militia equipment and took their places. The siren rings when a plane passes into a zone of 50 kilometers around Hanoi; loudspeakers alert the population, followed by the siren and then the all-clear sign. We have not been able to detect the sound of American planes, though in several alerts we heard Vietnamese Air Force planes. Over 2 days already I find myself resisting the sound of the alert—the city seems to go on about its business, and it is

---

[28] Ernesto "Che" Guevara was an Argentine-born revolutionary and physician in Cuba whose economic ideas were embraced by Fidel Castro in the mid-1960s. Thomas E. Skidmore and Peter H. Smith, *Modern Latin America,* 4th ed. (New York: Oxford University Press, 1997), 283–86.

easy to forget that each alert, as likely as not, means a bomb dropped some-where (although the alert is also triggered by reconnaissance planes).

It is going to be difficult to see things informally. Our request for "cul-ture" turned into an official evening of entertainment. But we are aware of the need to be insistent about some spontaneity—for example, seeing a street dance. And we have been surprised about the relatively relaxed response of the Peace Committee to our taking off alone on walks. Some evening we will have to steer our way towards street theater or whatever. We will also improve, I think, our ability to draw out significant informa-tion through casual questions—in the car, while walking. Oanh is the best example: sometimes a question well placed triggers an unexpected flood of words. I'm working hard to know how to ask such questions, and when.

Saturday afternoon. Visit to Bao Tong Quan Doi (Museum of the Vietnam-ese People's Army), housed in what was formerly a French signal center. There are 3 parts to the museum:

1. 1930–1945. Armed forces until the 1945 Revolution.
2. 1945–1954. Resistance against French colonialists.
3. 1954–present
   a. armed political struggle against U.S. aggression
   b. DRV struggle against present air war

The museum also contains a courtyard display of wreckage of all types of American aircraft, except B-52's. (We had an air alert while seeing this part of the exhibit—an ironic twist—again could not hear U.S. planes.) We were shown the 1953–54 phase of the French resistance, with most of the time given to Dien Bien Phu. The feature attraction was an enormous room, with a 3-D model of the battle, with electrical lights pointing out step-by-step stages of the battle, accompanied by an unintelligible recorded expla-nation in English. We then saw several rooms of photos of the struggle pres-ently in the south and the north. The emphasis on Dien Bien Phu is significant: that part of the display was clearly built for the Vietnamese as a very crucial part of their history. But its emphasis for us seemed to suggest two things: one, it dramatized the fact that the Vietnamese won then, and that now they are winning (the official line of the Bratislava conference and the main point of the new NLF program); and, two, it may suggest that U.S. troops in all of South Vietnam are essentially going to meet a Dien Bien Phu.

This message will be carried to us again and again, and it is not by accident, we are sure, that the day began with a visit to a pagoda and ended with a long account of Dien Bien Phu. (And, even later, the most recent documentary films.)

Dinner, Saturday: a joyous, drunken affair. Much Vietnamese food (excellent!) with the Peace Committee, Vietnamese friends from Bratislava (Pham Hong, Nguyen Minh Vy), and some new people: Mrs. Phan Thi An from the Women's Union, and Tien Phong from the Students' Union. I am no longer surprised when I meet someone who already knows my name and what I do (it happens regularly). Dinner was filled with merriment, some serious toasting, and too much liquor (which, I think, even affected Tam and Toan). But business is business: it was clear when the meal was over, and we were promptly ushered into the hall for 3 documentary films—one of them, about the youth/militia, very impressive . . . and to bed, to arise to go to the Museum of the Revolution at 6:00 a.m.

(Air alerts, Saturday, 3:00?)

Hanoi, Day 3: Sunday, October 1. Museum of the Revolution; evening, Song and Dance Ensemble

Sunday, 1 October 1967 (written late evening—
have we only been here two full days??)

First impression: so many little things happened today, all day. Quick impressions: we are like old friends—revealing conversations took place more and more easily (Tom said more has been said in 2 days than in the 2 weeks when he visited in 1965). It is amazing when I realize that I am walking around (almost easily) a country with which my government is at war. Feels like I've been here weeks—names come more easily, conversation flows, it becomes easier to say things on the spot, but mostly, so many little and large things are crammed into one day that it must really be a week.

The day began at 5:30 (tomorrow begins at 4:30 so I will stop in a moment and fall behind again), and a 6:00 a.m. trip to the Museum of the Revolution, built in 1959 as an educational institute for youth, and administered by the Ministry of Culture. In 30 rooms of display, the history moves from the earliest tradition, to the fight against French, to the 1945 revolution with a great emphasis on Ho Chi Minh, to the current times (resistance against the French till 1954, U.S. aggression, and a room about peace efforts).

At the Museum of the Revolution, October 1. FROM LEFT: *Vivian Rothstein, Carol McEldowney, and the director (photographer unknown).*

We learned also that there are smaller museums in various localities, and mobile exhibition teams also run by the Ministry of Culture.

Interesting highlights of what we saw: early history (1st room), first settlement as long ago as 2000 B.C. First signs of invasion (Chinese) date 202 B.C., copper arrows. 2nd room: early struggle against French colonialists and the Vietnamese mandarin feudalists, depicted quite graphically in a cartoon. Phan Dinh Phung (1847–1896) was an early hero who led the struggle against the French. 3rd room and those following were Ho Chi Minh rooms. The first had 2 large portraits above Ho—one of Lenin, the other of Marx. 4th room: French colonialists conceded Indochina to the Japanese fascists.

Revolution: 1945 over 2 million people starved. Ho returned to his fatherland in 1941, lived in Tac-Bo cave. The next year he left, was captured by Chiang Kai-shek and imprisoned (wrote Prison Diary).[29] Began to build the Vietnamese People's Army with 34 men and 13 rifles.

Many of the major events from 1945 on are depicted by glassed-in

---

[29] An English edition of Ho's Prison Diary was published in 1971. Ho Chi Minh, *The Prison Diary of Ho Chi Minh*, trans. Aileen Palmer, intro. Harrison E. Salisbury (New York: Bantam Books, 1971).

papier-mâché models—very effectively, for example, Ho's "orders" for the August 1945 uprising and the 19th August invasion of the Governor's Palace in Hanoi.

Later rooms: Dien Bien Phu. U.S. aggression in South and North Vietnam, very similar (some identical materials) to Museum of VPA. Finally, an excellent documentary of the life of Ho Chi Minh (interrupted by an air alert), which was also very cleverly a history (brief) of 3rd world movements and a social commentary on class problems and need for revolution in other countries. Examples: film clips of KKK[30] burnings in the U.S. and poverty in Manhattan; clips of misery in Paris; shots of international solidarity between Ho and African nations; and the defeat of the fascists in WWII. And all remarkably balanced by magnificent shots of Bac Ho[31] joyfully applauding and being surrounded by dancing and singing children.

Usual formality and gift presentation afterwards (I wrote the message from the American friends in the Museum book for visitors). It's hard to be prepared for those situations, even though we know they are coming. I feel a little better about speaking spontaneously, but I also have a feeling that I want to be sincere, want to avoid the corny, propaganda-sounding remarks—largely important so I will be conditioned to talk in real terms to real people back home, away from the unreality suggested by being here (that is, unreality about language used).

During lunch we had our 2nd air alert of the day, but only after another very revealing conversation with Xuan Oanh. He talked about the Peace Committee of the DRV (part of the World Peace Council)—how it arose, formed by intellectuals in 1950, governed by Congress of 85 people (not a mass organization), with government financial support. Peace Committees of Eastern European (and Western) socialist countries have been conservative forces, unwilling to take a stand on 3rd world resistance movements, and only being anti-bomb, peace treaty groups. The war in Vietnam has pushed them on this, and the World Peace Council has moved to the left. But Oanh exhibited considerable disdain for them—for socialist countries of Eastern Europe in general.

Talked also quite a bit about the area of communication. Each organization and part of the government in the DRV maintains an elaborate courier system from province to province, a technique begun during the French

---

[30] Ku Klux Klan, violent white supremacist group in the United States.
[31] "Uncle" Ho Chi Minh.

Vietnamese passages with translations (Vietnamese not in McEldowney's handwriting).

resistance and improved enormously since then. Messages of any import are relayed this way, and there is a careful check system. (Telephones are too dangerous—messages can be intercepted.) In the case of foreign visits, the Army must be notified of every move for security reasons. This doesn't explain decentralization, but it does explain in part both the time needed for decision-making and the emphasis on local areas finding their own ways to best implement general national policy. Communication methods are too time-consuming for anything else. All communication with the South, on the other hand, is done through the NLF, and a constantly changing code is used over a wireless transmitter.

The afternoon was a remarkable experience. I did two very different things: took a walk alone with Vivian, and got fitted for pants. In order: first, just the surprise of being able to walk around alone in the city. I worried a little at first about air alerts, but realized we would just follow the population. We walked to the lake in the center of the city, sat on a bench for a while. Remarkably different from Phnom Penh—people here are curious about us, but don't approach us. Partly it's because they don't even know a few words of French or English (want a woman? etc.) but I'm sure it's also the intense Vietnamese pride. People do smile—shyly, warmly, a lot. It's one of the most dramatic characteristics of people here. A fine thing occurred; while we were sitting on the bench, a militia man, in uniform and carrying hats, suddenly stopped, walked over to us, and shook hands. Then we began to walk around the lake and slowly gathered an enormous crowd—kids, militia people, young guys and girls. I tried to talk French then used sign language and finally found someone who spoke a little English. We got ourselves pinned back against a rock with about 125 people surrounding us, and I tried to explain to our "translator" who we were. Hard—so hard—to say "I am an American" in that situation. They must hate us (imagine a German speaking to Americans on a street corner during World War II—he would've been lynched). It was difficult to know if we were acting properly, but I think we did okay—weren't insulting and satisfied people's curiosity a little. I was so affected, though, by being unable to say more than 3 words in Vietnamese. Nevertheless, the experience of drawing people together like that was unprecedented (and probably both safer and easier for two women). It made both Vivian and I wish for a walk with a woman interpreter.

In the afternoon Hieu and Toan took Vivian, Jock, and me to be fitted for trousers (at the "diplomatic store," which works fast). Hieu opened up a lot in that informal setting. He is originally from Saigon, but has been in the North many years, and is very much a city boy. He talked some about city-countryside differences, and we talked a little about women and their changing role in Vietnamese society. Most women now marry around 25, to men whose age is close; and they pick their own partners (equality and the right to free choice is in the constitution). Yet it seems clear that the role of women is undergoing constant change, and I am eager to find ways to explore this. Interesting conversation with Hieu about generosity of Vietnamese people—how true!

One possible project; talk to women at a clinic or hospital about birth control (with a woman interpreter if possible). Or try to talk with some of the women at the hotel whose work clearly extends beyond waitress (Minh Tinh) or barmaid (Pham dai Hai).

The evening was a perfectly joyful occasion. We were treated to a very special performance of the Nhā hāt ca múa Nhac Viêtnam (song and dance house of Vietnam), a large ensemble (40 people?) just returned from the front lines near the 17th parallel. The costumes, music, instruments, and particularly the spirit were truly inspirational. A tour of the U.S. by this group would end the war—exquisitely done—so tasteful, yet so revolutionary. A list of the numbers:

1. Women's group: 9 women, with 16-string instrument.
2. "Bring the Paddies to the Street" and "Quang Binh"—province song,—patriotic!
3. Monochord and orchestra—a very haunting instrument: lyrical, poignant, yet strong "for the South."
4. Monochord and orchestra: American folksong (unidentified).
5. Female solo and accordion: "My Love Do Not Go Back"— folksong of the North.
6. Female solo and accordion: "Les Fleurs de Pó Lang"—tale of small girl.
7. Flute solo and ensemble (beautiful!)—"Good Harvest in Our Native Land."
8. Part of folk opera: daughter of rich peasant flirts with a Buddhist monk—supposed to be "anti-feudal"—delightful dance and costume.
9. Solo with ensemble: "Horse on the Long March."
10. Woman's voice: "Beat the Drums Up"—popular at Chinese-Vietnamese frontier.
11. Women's group again: song of militia girls in the northwest singing while U.S. aircraft is downed.

12. Song of solidarity between the army and people—2 string guitar. Popular in north and central Vietnam.
13. Drum solo and ensemble. Brilliant! with a variety of sparkling instruments.
14. Male solo with accordion: American folksong (Red River Valley?).
15. Male solo with accordion: "The Elephant Song." Singer is absolutely Caruso-like in style and stage presence—hilarious!
16. Song and dance of Vietnamese minorities—central area. Main instruments: 3 women on trung (bamboo tubes), man on flute, man on bells (gongs). And 8 women dancers. Costumes are exquisite and the music and dance sheer poetry.
17. Same group: song of girl making bamboo spikes while dreaming of the countryside being liberated.

After the performance we talked a while with the troupe who were eager, as everyone else, to hear of anti-war activities. I was struck again, in particular, by their response to Vivian and me—eagerness to meet women.

The other highlight of the evening was Hieu's bringing his wife, Chi, and 5-year-old daughter, Hien, to the performance, as well as Oanh's 5-year-old son, Chi. There was something very close and warm about that—they all exposed a very different part of themselves (Oanh even smiled and said that son #3 was by mistake). (Tom said nothing like that ever happened in the entire 2 weeks he was here.) I hope I will get to see more of Chi [Hieu's wife], who also works for the Peace Committee, but as a translator of written documents.

Hanoi, Day 4: Monday, October 2. Hanoi War Crimes Tribunal Committee; visits to bombed sites; evening, walk around city, Hanoi Information Center

Monday, October 2, 1967

No time to sleep. Another full day (although not enough to do). Got up at 5 to meet with Hanoi War Crimes Tribunal Committee, back at 8 for breakfast, out again after 2:30 meeting with them, back at 6:30, and several hours into the streets with Hieu and Tam; finally nightcap at the bar with Hieu, Oanh, and to bed—to try to stop thinking long enough to sleep.

We spent the morning seeing bombed schools (university level) in Ha

Dong province, about 8 km.from Hanoi. (For some reason, followed by a peaceful stop at a historic pagoda, built 1010—Quan Thanh Temple, with a rich legendary history about a god-sent prince to administer ghosts, and a Chinese prince who didn't want to become king. Peculiar psychology—why such a stop?)

Some general comments:

Policy of school dispersal was announced soon after first bombing of the North. And it was speeded up in 1965. The city had begun building—and following new city plan—1954–1960. Many schools were built in a concentrated area—and this has been public information. This building (of schools, workers' quarters, etc.) has been on Hanoi's outskirts (rather than central city).

Yet U.S. explanation for all these bombings was "military installations or barracks." Several buildings were hit precisely, and pellet bombs were in great evidence. The reason for the U.S. bombing is not necessarily clear. But my speculation is that the U.S. knew these buildings were evacuated, knew they are (were) part of an important thrust forward in DRV life (advanced education for the youth cadres of the nation), and therefore symbolically become the best targets to bomb—destroy the signs of socialist progress—and the training grounds for new leadership. If the U.S. thought the buildings were in use, did they know they are schools? And were the targets deliberate? Why one particular building rather than another? Were any of the targets unplanned?

Afternoon: began with introduction by Nguyen Dut Hanh, of Hanoi War Crimes Tribunal Committee.

Highlights on Hanoi history: Established 1010. Since 1954 the political, economic, cultural center of the DRV. Has been changed from consumption capital to production capital. (Production increased ten times between 1955 and 1965.)

(All contained in written report we were given. no.1)[32]

---

[32] In several places in the journal McEldowney refers to written reports the delegation received from the North Vietnamese. These reports were not found in the journal.

Name of school Location, Date Built	Date of bombing and time	No. of students	No. buildings	Nature of bombing; damage	Injuries	U.S. explanation; other comments
Bó Thuy Loi School for Water Conservation; 1961	5-12-67 5-22-67 (noon)	2,000	16	CBU; rockets; explosives. Large crater; several buildings razed.	None	Had been evacuated already, though still some used. U.S. claimed military barracks.
Broadcasting Technical School; 1961	5-12-67 5-22-67 (noon)	1,500	24	CBU; rockets; explosives. Large craters	no casualties	Laboratory & transformer razed. Already evacuated. (Barracks)
Foreign Language Complementary School ("improvement courses"); 1960	5-12-67: 4 p.m. 5-22-67: 10 a.m.	2,000+	18	1 large building, bombed hard	1 killed 2 wounded	Many there when bomb hit but escaped to shelter. 1 building destroyed
General College, Social Science Faculty of University of Hanoi	5-12-67 5-22-67	3,000+	8	Many CBU- pellet bombs; large crater 6–7 meters deep (750 lb. bomb); office destroyed	none	Had already been evacuated
College for National Minorities (people trained for teaching, political and administrative positions)	5-12-67	1,500	?	Rockets; CBU. Dormitory destroyed; library with 5,000 volumes destroyed	none	Already evacuated
Trade Union School; built 1961 Dong Da District, 3 km from hotel	12-14-66	1,200	4	Rocket—CBU. Lecture hall hit	5 killed 11 wounded	Had been evacuated, but still used. On same day Chinese and Romanian embassies also rocketed

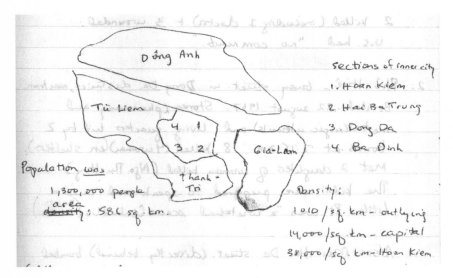

Sketch of Hanoi districts.

17 April 1966—first attacks on Hanoi, preceded by many reconnaissance flights; intensive bombing till November 1966 on densely populated targets (including dike on Red River).

2 December 1966, first strike against central city.

Explosives used: CBU (fragmentation); high pressure. (Example: bomb on dike 3,000 pounds, created crater 9 mt. deep and 12 mt. wide; 1,000 people needed for repair work.)

Bomb damage we visited:
1. Hospital in Hoan Kiem part of Hanoi (built 1954). Bombed 21 August 1967, at noon. Located ½ km. from hotel, next to Cathedral. Hit by 3 planes, a strike missile the 2nd time. Cubic pellets were released. (Got a sample.) Equipment was destroyed. 2 killed (including 1 doctor) and 3 wounded. U.S. had "no comment."
2. Phô Húê—busy street in Dong Da district, near tram. Bombed 22 August 1967. Stores (pharmacy and metallurgic utensils) and living quarters hit by 2 bombs at 7:15 a.m. 8 killed (4 women) (in shelters). Met 2 daughters of woman killed (Nga Thi Hang). The kids were prepared to speak and cried a little. It was a wretched scene (called us aunts and uncles).
   Also: Mai Hac De Street (directly behind) bombed same time and

day. 3 houses were razed, many others damaged. 4 children in a shelter were killed and 7 others wounded. While looking around, we heard sad mournful music. . . .

At both sites we were escorted by Mrs. Pham Kim Hy, a member of the Hai Ba Trung district Hanoi War Crimes Investigating Committee. (She also serves on her local district administrative committee.) The War Crimes Committee, formed in 1966, now has local representatives in every district. It is clear that the DRV has invested a lot of faith and energy in the Tribunal. . . .

3. Phu Xa village (part of Phu Thuong commune in Tu Liem district)—72 families (360 people, Catholics). Bombed 13 August 1966 (4 km. north of Hanoi) 12 noon: 4 CBU's (2,560 pellets or 7/person) and 2 high pressure bombs. 24 (10 children 2–13 years old) killed: 23 wounded.

Visited the village, which was rebuilt in 20 days: Catholic Church rebuilt, new trees planted, and people stayed on the land. We met Mrs. Le Thi Huong, whose whole family (4) was killed. She was very clear about their hatred of the U.S. aggressor.

The People's Council and administrative committee of Phu Thuong commune, with the aid of Thuy Phuong commune, have constructed a monument on the spot of the house whose family of 8 was killed, and have built a "hatred house" to store evidence of U.S. war crimes in the area. Similar museums have been built in other parts of DRV.

We received reports of the bombing on Hanoi proper on 2 December 1966. Targets included Vietnam-Polish Friendship School, Ty Ky and Phap Van pagodas, Hoang Liet and other villages in Thanh Tri district.

Other bombing December 13th and 14th, 1966: same target as December 2nd, especially Hoang Liet village. December 14, 1966: in Hoan Kiem district, most populous, several streets bombed: Phuc Tan and Nguyen Thiep (1 km. from hotel). Both streets: 14 killed and 20 wounded. Diplomatic missions—Chinese and Romanian,—bombed the same day. 1966 Hanoi casualty figures: 289 killed or wounded (including 105 children under 15 years, and 82 women).

1967 bombings: Hanoi
25 April 1967: Dong Anh district (hospital, senior high school, several communes); and Gia Lam district (civilian airport) (20 F-105s). Also April

Phu Xa "Hatred House," October 2. FROM LEFT: *guide, Vivian Rothstein, Norman Fruchter, and Carol McEldowney (photographer unknown).*

26, 28, 29 (total April: 176 bombs). 52 CBU's = 30,000 pellets, 58 killed, 154 wounded.

May 4, 5, 12, 13, 14, 19, 20, 21, 22, 1967
June 10, 1967
August 11: Long Bien Bridge
August 12
August 22: Phô Húê in Dong Da area (main street)
August 23: Thanh Tri hospital

In general, it is argued the attacks are deliberate for 3 reasons:
1. U.S. has many reconnaissance planes and know what they are hitting. (Not very convincing, since the Vietnamese also tend to discount reliability of U.S. reconnaissance and <u>we</u> know it is not that accurate nor does the U.S. have enough translators of constantly changing film.)
2. U.S. planes dive in and fly low enough to aim. (This is reasonable, although given the effectiveness of self-defense rifle units, it would seem that many more planes flying low would be hit.)

3. Certain targets have been hit repeatedly. (This is the most convincing argument to me. Regardless of what explanation the U.S. gives about these targets, they <u>have</u> been hit over and over again and quite systematically in some areas.)

After dinner: delightful walk about the city, with Hieu and Tam. Highlights: information center of Hanoi with variety of interesting propaganda features: photos of U.S. anti-war protests and riots (very dated, with some pretty poor captions); maps and charts showing U.S. planes downed with district scoreboards. Yet an important place with many people looking at different news items. The city seems effectively organized in this respect: it is filled with scoreboards of American planes downed, and propaganda/information displays, which people <u>do</u> seem to read.

- Listened to an old woman folksinger—learned that many such people are blind or invalids and make their money this way. If they don't have enough, their local administrative councils are responsible for them (and other jobless people).
- Sampled local ice cream.
- Talked to a "man on the street"—not substantively.
- Saw tiny kids in the middle of the street making planes and tanks out of clay.
- More revealing conversations with Hieu about customs and behavior—he's a terribly sentimental guy (and perfectly lovely). He talked, perhaps a little wistfully, of youth as the vanguard and for the need of love and friendship especially during war.

Again—that strange feeling of wandering around the streets of Hanoi at night—a country at war—yet life seems to go on so normally.

No air alerts today.

Hanoi, Day 5: Tuesday, October 3. Visit to evacuated
factory outside Hanoi; Trade Union Federation

Tuesday, 3 October 1967

Trade Union Day

Morning: We were taken to an evacuated factory, perhaps 15 km. from Hanoi. A small part of a large small-machine-parts (engineering) factory, originally built with USSR aid, and evacuated 2 years ago. Most dramatically: we walked into what appeared to be thatched huts, to find humming (heavy) machines, sunk in cement, going full force. Modern equipment, in the middle of the countryside, with production moving along smoothly. I don't know what my image had been of an "evacuated factory" but this was not it! This was the first time the workshop had foreign visitors, and we received a grand welcome, with flowers, food, music (long array of patriotic songs); and many "big people" including a whole variety of officials (labor heroes, party leaders, youth organization people, Trade Union people). Even Hieu was surprised at the extent of the reception. Key report from Nguyen Dai Lôc—overall Director: factory has met its state plans yearly, with several labor heroes (2); (a title, we discovered, is approved by the National Assembly); 111 model workers (elected by the factory); and 4 units and 2 workshops with honorary degree of "socialist units." A very complex incentive system which still is not clear to me.

30% of staff is women. The factory has its own defense unit (we had an air alert there and for the first time heard U.S. bombs) and one star unit; workers have rifles by their sides.

Workers have been inspired by patriotism and the "Emulation Movement" to compete for more quality production at lower costs (Trade Union movement). Also has its own school which trains engineers, technical workers, and people for other factories.

Organization of all this is not yet clear. Factory workers do live in nearby villages and are part of commune administrative system. But it is clear that the factories also have a life unto themselves.

Lunch time back at the hotel: saw my first anti-aircraft missile—heard it before the alert sounded—looked like white smoke streaking through the air. It was reported to be a reconnaissance plane—not sure yet if it was hit.

Afternoon: meeting with Trade Union people, later followed by banquet dinner with them.

Finally, through a dinner discussion with Nguyen Minh, I vaguely got an idea of the Trade Union structure.

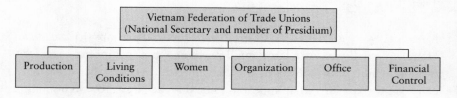

Each of 6 branches exists nationally.

There are 14 different Trade Unions; teachers, mechanical workers, health workers, etc. have their own unions, each within a district. For example:

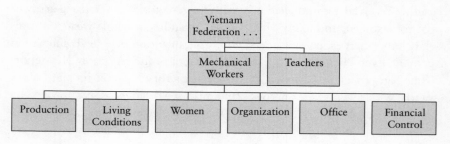

(And each group, e.g., teachers, is organized nationally.)

Each union has a division corresponding to the 6 national branches listed above: production, etc.

Still unclear is the role of the Party in all this, although for the first time there was explicit acknowledgement of the Party's role in "educating people to the proper consciousness." The relationship between the Trade Union, the Party, and the national state plan and how it operates on the local level is completely intricate. There are several layers of organization and several "movements."

In general, since the evacuation of many factories, stabilization has occurred. There has been special emphasis on production of farm implements to help guarantee adequate food supplies. One recent drive is the "Movement to Develop Initiative and Increase Labor Productivity during Warfare" (not clear whose movement).

Each factory has 2 teams:

1. Production team: discusses problems of management, production, which relate to specific profession, and not necessarily solvable by "political cadres."[33] The head, second head, and several workers are appointed by factory managing board. This is part of the movement to encourage workers' participation in factory management; and insure protection of machines and workers, and quality. Above factory level, how is this organized?

2. Trade Union Team: union members working in that organization. Head and vice-head are elected. These teams work closely with production teams.

There is also a workshop Party committee. The Party provides leadership along a mass line (education and persuasion) for workers in general, and for the production and trade union teams (although it respects suggestions of both). The Party's task is to raise consciousness of the workers, and several people were rather direct in using that phrase and speaking of the need for socialism.

All workers (laborers, professionals) are part of the Trade Unions. And public health workers play an important role. Several people at the afternoon meeting were medical people and we acquired a lot of information.

Dr. Anh Hoa (originally a Southerner who went to France in 1952 and returned to the North in 1962) is a pediatrician at Bach Mai Polyclinic. Dr. Quy is the head (also a woman) of Hoan Kiem hospital (bombed recently—21 August 1967).

The motto of the Public Health system, under Dr. Pham Ngoc Thach, is "Prevention First." Medical workers are prepared all over the country for a long-term struggle. Significant progress has taken place in research, prevention, response to the war, childcare. . . .

The Public Health service has organized a national network, inspired by the campaign to intensify care during the war. In the countryside, each

---

[33] Cadres, according to the U.S. government's *Area Handbook for North Vietnam* (1967), "comprise[d] a limited number of skilled officials highly indoctrinated in Party ideology and policies and trained in the art of bureaucratic management. . . . There [were], for example, administrative or state cadres (roughly equivalent to civil servants), propaganda cadres, management cadres, financial cadres, inspection cadres, Party cadres within the Party or the armed forces, intellectual cadres, educational cadres and so on." Harvey H. Smith et al, *Area Handbook for North Vietnam* (Washington, D.C.: Government Printing Office, 1967), 178.

Trade Union meeting, October 3. FROM LEFT: *Vivian Rothstein; Dr. Quy, head of Hoan Kiem Hospital; Carol McEldowney; wife of killed electrician; Dr. Anh Hoa, pediatrician (photographer unknown).*

province, district, village, hamlet, and cooperative has a medical cadre. In the cities each street quarter has a public health station, and medical workers are sent to individual homes as well. There is also a growing number of non-professional hygiene workers in various localities. Workplaces, such as factories, have public health workers on their production teams. First-aid networks are widespread; and surgery exists even on the village level.

The health system uses 2 approaches:

1. <u>Educational</u> work: emphasis on hygiene, within the family and the surroundings. There are frequently special drives or "attacks." The current campaign is "Hygiene against U.S. Aggression for National Salvation." There are also drives for women's health, with the establishment of "Sanitary" or "Menstrual" houses.
2. Actual medical prevention: particularly yearly inoculations against typhoid, polio, diphtheria, cholera, tetanus. Hanoi can boast of having experienced <u>no</u> epidemic in the last 6 years.

Research:

1. The war has greatly reduced importation of medicines and drugs, and Vietnam medical researchers have had to develop medicines

using domestic materials. For example, a material from the native lacquer tree has been used successfully to cure tapeworm, a common children's disease in tropical lands.

2. Substitute food products are also being researched. For example, milk has always been imported in quantity before the war. Researchers are now developing a substance from fish powder (in local great abundance) to provide the nutritional value of milk, especially for children under 1 year.

Continued discussion over dinner with Nguyen Minh about health, and particularly about birth control. There has been a great drive in the city and countryside to reduce family size. National average has declined from 6 children per family to 2.7 (not sure if this is city or national figure actually). There are picture exhibitions and classes all over Hanoi. The Youth Organization instructs men, and the Women's Union teaches women. Many contraceptive methods are used.

We spoke some about the "morality" issues of birth control. Information is readily available to married women but Minh insisted that single women "have no right" to need such information. After a frustrating discussion about sexual double standards, in which Minh insisted that colonial behavior has been eliminated, we reached some meeting of the minds. He also described one of the Youth Organization drives: the "3 Postponements."

1. when studying, postpone love
2. when loving, postpone marriage
3. when marrying, postpone having family

Also met, at Trade Union meeting, Le Trung Thanh, of the Vietnamese-Polish Friendship School, bombed 50 times, who described something about school preparedness for bombing. Often lives of many children are saved because

1. teachers are courageous in saving students
2. children themselves are brave
3. first-aid work right after bombing is very important and effective

To continue preparedness:

1. more shelters being built
2. sub-surface classes continue while schools are reconstructed

Hanoi, September 29–October 17, 1967　　　　47

Problems being studied (and solved):
1. need for lighter laboratory equipment (chemistry and physics) for transporting
2. transportation of children to evacuated schools
3. outfitting children with straw hats, first-aid kits, and kerosene lamps for night study

Not sure how much of a model this school is, but the point was made that in spite of the bombing, performance has improved (increased classes from 14 to 18; 10th grade graduates went from 90% to 93.7%, and 42% climb in number of students in the school).

Other miscellaneous information acquired from Thanh:

Food: There have been some experiments towards replacing the rice staple with bread. This is for "mobility" for people whose work makes cooking difficult. Wheat is imported in large quantities from socialist countries for this purpose. Typical family eats 2 meals daily: soup, fish, and rice are the basic staples. Breakfast is generally just coffee. Sometimes there is more food (fish, soup). Lunch meal is bread, soup, and tea (ché). Dinner meal is rice, vegetables, maybe soup, maybe fish, and "ché."

Food patterns don't vary greatly from city to countryside. Fruits and some vegetables seem to be abundant all over. (French patterns have certainly influenced banquets, etc., but local cuisine dominates.) It's common to walk about and see many people eating their meals on the street, and many people selling their goods, as well. Still necessary to learn about food rationing—amounts, which products, how regulated, etc.

Retirement: The average age of factory workers is strikingly young. 70% of them are less than 30 years. Retirement is at 60 years for men and 50 years for women. Didn't find out yet about retirement payments, pensions, etc. (Our trip to the evacuated factory was not very useful in giving us a view of the workers' lives.)

Hanoi, Day 6: Wednesday, October 4. Meeting with
cabinet officials and Colonel Ha Van Lau about bombing;
Hanoi Surgical Hospital; weapons exhibition

4 October 1967, Wednesday

2 air alerts within 15 minutes after breakfast and before leaving. Then into the fullest day yet:
1. surprise visit with 2 cabinet ministers, Pham Ngoc Thach and Pham Van Bach, and Colonel Ha Van Laû from War Crimes Committee
2. meeting with hospital people—medical crimes
3. press conference about school bombing
4. weapons exhibition by War Crimes Committee

Many significant discussions and thoughts. First, interview with Pham Ngoc Thach, Head of Public Health, member of Central Committee of War Crimes Investigating Team, formerly chairman of Saigon-Cholon Youth Resistance; and Pham Van Bach, Head of DRV Supreme Court (was president of Ham Bo—near Saigon—administrative committee) and important Party member. Colonel Ha Van Laû, Secretary and standing member of Investigation Committee (formerly head of Vietnamese liaison delegation post-Geneva) and also from the South. (Half of the DRV Cabinet members, as well as Pham Van Dong, originally were from the South.)

We posed 3 questions:
1. DRV interpretation of intention of U.S. bombing: reasons for certain targets. Method of terror?
2. U.S. at military crisis because bombing has failed. What will be next stage of escalation, and what is DRV's preparedness?
3. Recent data on bombing.

Long, probably important answer from Colonel Laû.
1. <u>Purpose and intention of U.S. bombing</u>: U.S. arguments: U.S. is protecting South Vietnam against aggression by North Vietnam. North is sending troops, violating Geneva Agreement. No mention of Vietnam fighting war of self-defense. Actual <u>long-range purpose</u> has to do with the nature of U.S. imperialism; U.S. wants to dominate the world under banner of anti-communism, and to do this must interfere in the affairs of other nations. Much attention has

been given to Southeast Asia, especially since the founding of the PRC [People's Republic of China] after WWII.

U.S. plan was to first dominate Indochina and then the world. Step-by-step plan (1) U.S. directly entered Indochina in 1954 by aiding French colonialists in their repression. But U.S. was defeated by Dien Bien Phu, the Geneva Agreements, and creation of DRV. (2) Occupation of South Vietnam, to use it as springboard and neo-colonialist military base. (3) Next step would be to occupy North Vietnam, then Laos and Cambodia.

Actuality: in the South the U.S. failed 1954–1961. Special warfare was launched in 1961, defeated 1964–65. U.S. switched to local warfare (ground forces), which it had been reluctant to do since its experience in Korean War. Political efforts and special warfare both failed; ground forces is current strategy.

Attack on the North is part of U.S. plan to occupy the South—strategy is to aggress against North Vietnam as a way of occupying the South. (Part of Staley-Taylor plan.)[34] U.S. expected the DRV to be defeated easily, to come to conference table willingly, and "give" the South to the U.S. as separate country (in violation of Geneva). (U.S. of course did not expect such resistance.)

2. Nature of escalation: First, U.S. greatly misjudged capacity of DRV, which has dealt deathly blows. U.S. special warfare strategic offensives (1965–1966 and 1966–1967) have failed, threatening total defeat. Therefore, U.S. intensifies bombing of North to bring pressure to the South.

   a. Geographical Stages: movement from southern to northern and western to eastern provinces, movement from far from Hanoi/Haiphong to outskirts to central city. By August 1967, most populous Hanoi streets bombed.

   b. Intensity and scale—weapons:

      1. more night attacks; increased daily missions; previously single attacks—now repeated attacks on same target.

      2. nature of equipment escalation; before: Air Force, 7th Fleet;

---

[34] Eugene A. Staley was an economist from Stanford University who traveled to Vietnam in 1961 and produced an unofficial report. Maxwell Taylor, retired army chief of staff, was brought back into service in 1961 by John F. Kennedy to deal with Vietnam issues and to head Joint Chiefs of Staff. JFK Library, Boston.

now: Navy's role increasing; addition of B-52s; addition of long-range artillery stations in South Vietnam.

3. conventional weaponry: ability to kill people has increased. Before: (pineapple) pellet bombs were used, but many not exploding. Now: pineapple delayed bombs, much more dangerous. Explosives: weight increased to 3,000 pounds (larger than WWII); development of delayed time.
4. use of banned weapons—napalm; magnesium; most recently, phosphorus; toxic chemicals—which kill crops and people (recently used in Vinh Linh). No toxic gases in North yet.

c. Tactics of escalation very intentional. U.S. boast of reconnaissance and precision aircraft. Targets often hit precisely, within 20 meter margin. Not a mistake. When U.S. repeatedly hits schools, hospitals, churches, dikes, it is clear civilians are main target. Also trying to sow religious dissent. Cities and populated areas are hit (including Hanoi and Haiphong): 30 provincial townships have been attacked; of 97 district townships, 60 attacked (of which 10 were razed). Countless villages, especially near the DMZ [demilitarized zone] , have been hit hard. (Alert came, but we continued.)

U.S. hits communication lines: to keep people from going South and because repair work needs ½ million (and they, therefore, cannot help South Vietnam). But U.S. is fighting genocidal war. Nature of DRV resistance to U.S. aggression. It is people's war—the whole population of DRV must be mobilized in economy, culture, military, social.

There have been losses, but in general the building of a socialist society (which fights aggression with spirit) has been speeded up. The dispersal of the city population to the countryside has been increased; industrial output has grown; agricultural crops are better. Air defense is effective on all levels and altitudes: self-defense militias with rifles at low altitudes; anti-aircraft missiles—middle altitudes; and SAM (surface to air missiles, Russian) for high altitudes.

Future prospect? Johnson still trying to defeat North to subdue main front (South). Since Johnson wants victory and re-election, he will not withdraw and will continue to escalate as failure increases. Vietnam prepared to confront (1) increased air war through air and navy, (2) ground forces to the North. (On question of A-bombs, would be absolutely suicidal to use them.)

<u>Conclusion</u>: must explain to American people that peace must come with independence and freedom. (Also willing to meet again with us.)

In the afternoon (after 4th air alert) we visited the <u>Hanoi Surgical Hospital</u> and got another of many reports which are beginning to become a well-established pattern: greetings; glad to welcome American friends; list of data and evidence (this time given to us afterwards in printed form); we know the difference between the aggressors and the friends. Interpretation, of course, is a problem—language really becomes stale. People present were Pham Van Thu, Director of the Hospital and probably a party man, and a doctor (one of the few people I've met here who is absolutely arrogant in style).

Discussion was a list of achievements (to 1965), especially since 1954.
1. Personal: doctor/patient ratio from 1/180,000 to 1/200.
2. Facilities: hospitals in 90% of districts; sanitary stations in villages (mostly hygiene and vaccination); dispensaries for maternity and malaria; health services for factories. (Were told number of hospitals doubled from March 1965 to March 1966.)
3. Epidemics wiped out or under control: cholera, smallpox, polio, typhoid fever.
4. Elimination of social diseases: TB, malaria, trachoma, leprosy.
5. Improved <u>maternity</u> care: reduced maternal mortality rate (now 4/1000) and pre-natal (now 26/1000).
See Report #2—public health in the DRV, pp.7–10.[35]

Following was a list and description (with photos) of bombing of hospitals and health facilities.

Since the bombing began in 1965, to 30 August 1967, 127 hospitals have been wiped out, as well as some drugstores, medical training school, drug factory. See statement #3.[36] Among most serious were:
1. Quynh Lap Leper Sanitorium: June 1965 (already written about extensively), about 6 km. from Route 1, near the coast.
2. Thanh Hoa TB Hospital—large research center, July 1965.
3. Yen-Bai Province: July 1965, entire medical service destroyed.

---

[35] Report not included in the journal.

[36] Statement not included in the journal.

Then met 4 recent victims:

1. Ta Quoc Cuong (8 yr old boy): hit 22 August 1967 at Phó Hue. Brain wound—may have permanent psychological effect.
2. Nguyen Tien Hiuh (16 yr old boy): both legs paralyzed from crushed vertebrae—still no sensation but operation successful.
3. Nguyen Thi Kim Tuyen (18 yr old girl): hit 16 August 1967 by pellet in spinal cord. Better now—but legs both still paralyzed.
4. Cong Thi Ty (56 yr old woman): hit 5 May 1967 by pellet in brain (unremovable). I felt the soft skull. Awful.

Most interesting was description of new treatment methods for war damages:

1. Bone treatment: after operation, bamboo tape with native substance is put on <u>outside</u> of wound (instead of a plaster cast). The bone regenerates (in ½ the time of western method) and is not shortened at all.
2. Burn treatment: curing time is less because of local method using bacillus subtilis (lime water?).

Finally, the usual summary about growth of facilities, quality of care, production of medicines in spite of war. The medical cures discovered do seem amazing, as does the research being done on food substitutes, etc. (Tallies to date in North Vietnam: 78 medical workers killed, and 35 wounded; and 262 patients killed, and 242 wounded.)

Later—same afternoon—given over to latest accounts of bombing on <u>schools</u>. We were rushed to a press conference called by the Ministry of Education, cooperation from War Crimes Committee people, at International Press Club. Speakers: Nguyen Van Huyen, Minister of Education, gave statement (see #4) and Han Sun Huy, Director of recently bombed Ha Phu School (Thanh Hoa), spoke.

The bombed village is 8 km. from Rte. 1, 10 km. from the coast, and is comprised of 3 hamlets. The bombed hamlet is clearly agricultural: 200 by 300 meters area, with 354 households and 1,281 people; 254 kids in the primary school and 151 in 7th level.

The press conference described the bombing in great detail, with maps, photos, sample pellets, and books. The feature was 2 small kids, both injured: a young boy, still in fever, with a bandaged head; and a little girl (8 yr.) who told the story. It was awful—poor damn kid. Of course, the trans-

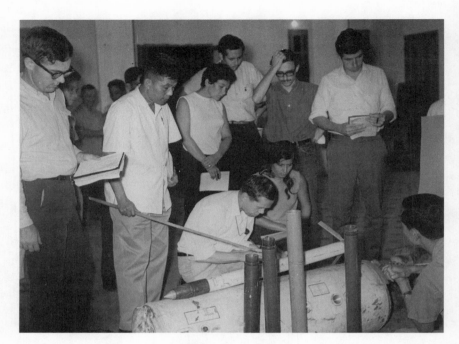

Delegation visiting weapons exhibition, October 4, evening. STANDING
FROM LEFT: *Rennie Davis, guide, Vivian Rothstein, Bob Allen, Norman
Fruchter, Tom Hayden;* KNEELING: *Jock Brown, Carol McEldowney (photographer unknown).*

lation (poor Hieu) was a nightmare, and the whole scene was unpleasant.
(I felt like any other stony-faced journalist.) Long debate afterwards about
whether the kid was rehearsed, how staged it was, etc. My own feeling was
that it was not practiced necessarily, but exploitative nonetheless, and I
wasn't very moved by it.

It was clear also that our hosts had requested our presence (in the morning, the Tribunal people made certain we would attend). Many journalists
there were delighted at the presence of the American delegation and we
rapidly became the target of conversations and cameras after the press conference officially ended.

Evening: Weapons Exhibition
Turned out to be one of the most interesting sessions yet. War Crimes
people spent a lot of time with us and they clearly did some special prepa-

rations, and to our surprise Pham Van Bach stayed throughout the entire evening. Not clear why they attached such time and importance to this.

Dong Ai—head of subcommittee of weapons used, gave a general introduction. Also present: Dr. Le Thi Chung, specialist in incendiary weapons, burn treatment; Dr. Vu Ngoc Thu, medical legalities; and Le Duc Tiet, chemical weapons.

Exhibition is set up to deal with 3 types of weapons.

1. Classical or conventional weapons (not banned) used in genocidal manner (against populous areas, etc.). Used in mass quantities, against agricultural villages. Example: Vinh Duang in Vinh Linh province (DMZ). Between June 19th and 24th, 1967: 165 attacks, 3,700 bombs—over 617 households with 3,000 people. Area hit: 1,400,000 square meters (over 1 bomb per person). Used for terror.

   Samples: large variety of time bombs, up to 3,000 pounds. Some have surface explosions, other go deeply into the ground. Craters created vary from 22–26 meters wide and 7–9 meters deep (2,000 pound, largest used so far) to 24–28 meters wide and 8–10 meters deep (experimental 3,000 pound with tail). Smallest we saw is 250 pounds.

   Also saw strike missile (which releases cubic pellets), a variety of rockets (up to 19 can be sent at once), and "bullpup" air-to-ground (1,000 pound).

2. Weapons banned by international law. U.S. claim is that these are used for defoliation only, but they are being used against people and crops. Included are various chemicals. "Combat poisons" are used—these poison the air and force increased underground life. Used especially in South. Low-speed planes must fly at low altitudes and a stable fly line to drop these chemicals, which is why they have not been used in the North (air defense is too effective). These chemicals have been used:

   a. For crop destruction. 2-4-D, 2-4-5-T, C_aCN_2, DNOC, DOP are used. These are useful weed killers in tiny dosages, but enough is used in South Vietnam to seriously damage trees, animals, poultry, the soil itself, and sometimes people.

   b. Chemicals used on people are DM (adansyth), CN and CS (mixture). Small amounts cause tears. 8/1000 milligrams/liter is unbearable. 3 mg/liter is death in 1 minute. These are carried in grenade-style containers (which, frighteningly enough) say "Riot" on it, or in tube-shaped containers. They are used by NCOs [Non-Commissioned Officers]. Also, is a launcher, knapsack-style, containing CS grenades, and lightable by a generator. (Saw samples of these.)

c. Napalm (used in the North and South): There are several varieties. NP (WWI) has been greatly improved. Now burns as hot as 2,000° C. NP_B (polythyron) is the most advanced, to be used massive. U.S. has announced plans to spend $35 million on its production and to use 720 pounds per day. What is DRV source of data here? Saw samples of Napalm sticking to walls, and many, many incredible photographs showing the effects of the burning. Especially dramatic effect on arms and legs: just completely distorts the edges of the bones.

d. White phosphorus: only tiny amount is needed. It burns readily, can continue burning 5–6 days, right through flesh. Quick death. Again, we saw samples and many photos.

e. Newest chemical is magnesium bomb: it and thermite have heat of 2,500 to 3,000° C. It has been dropped in the South, near Saigon (Bien Suc) on 18 January 1967 over 49 sq. km. The largest area ever hit by such heat, by B-52. Entire village was razed. Also dropped in the North, 16 January 1967, on Giao Chan, Giao Thuy district, in Nam Ha Province. (Denied by U.S.) Characteristically, all the chemicals have greater effect on children and older people whose bodies are not as strong as young adults'.

3. Experimental weapons, used in the South first, now in the North. Most important is the CBU—pellet bombs,—which are effective only on bodies. We saw wooden bars 2" in diameter which had stopped pellets. These were experimental at first and now are used on a large scale. Each mother bomb can have up to 600 bomblets (with many pellets); and each mother bomb describes a death area 250 meters wide by 1,000 meters long (250,000 sq. km.). We saw several extensive displays of the effects of various pellet bombs:

a. Global-shaped fragmentation bombs contained inside. Two halves of canister spins with centrifugal force, releasing a detonator inside. The canister carries 640 bomblets with 300 pellets each. A pellet can have the effect of a common cartridge. But, unlike a bullet, it can zigzag inside the body and not simply be diverted.

We saw preserved samples of an eye, brain, heart, and kidney which had experience zigzagging pellets. Pellets also create long splits in the bone. In spite of the amazing medical research being done in the DRV, it is clear that many shrapnel and wounds created by these weapons are untouched by current medical research.

Other things we saw included

b. butterfly bomb: explodes immediately on touching ground— carried in 30–60–90 mother bombs

c. 20mm cartridge, banned since WWI, which explodes <u>inside</u> the body (high explosive)

d. fragmentation bomb; 4 dispensers, case explodes on ground and releases (per dispenser) 250 pellets per bomb, total death area is 200 meters wide and 400–600 meters long.

Hanoi and Nam Ha Province, Days 7 and 8: Thursday and Friday, October 5–6. Preparations and trip to Nam Ha Province; bombing damage; underground factory

Thursday, 5 October 1967 [written 10-6-67]

Entire day spent preparing for our trip to the "locality." Only in the morning did we learn that in fact we were leaving for only one day, to Nam Ha Province. The reasons for that, of course, are not known to us—the whole decision-making process is rather a mystery. Oanh and Hieu did not come—why? Only one interpreter (a poor one) came. Did they know we would not talk to many "average folk"? Were they absolutely secure about our safety? Was Oanh in particular needed for other work? In the car Toan said that Colonel Ha Van Laû (Tribunal) had wanted us to go to Thanh Hoa Province, but the Peace Committee thought that was too dangerous. Wonder how decisions are made, once a group of Americans is here, about allocating our time. For example, if there had been military clearance for a Thanh Hoa trip, could Colonel Laû have insisted on that in spite of Peace Committee views? Does the Peace Committee consult with a sub-Cabinet group about who we see? How much autonomy does it have? Doesn't seem like it would, much more than usual Peace Committee in a socialist country.

We know very little about the Party, and they haven't told us much. Because we're not American Communist Party? Other reasons? But I want to find out—significance is obvious. Know only that estimated membership is 1.8 to 2 million, very high, with total population of 17 to 18 million. Cabinet ministers (Thach, Bach) are members, but which Trade Union people, for example, are?[37] Oanh might be, Hieu says he's hoping to become one. At the province we were greeted (first Phu Le and then Nam Ha) by a representative of the Foreign Relations Department, an entirely new entity to me. (Party?) And at the province meeting there was much more openness in acknowledging that we have here the "Central Committee of the Province and the administrative committee of the village." Furthermore, they said that people's spirit was great because we have Bac Ho, the Workers Party, the socialist countries' support, and support of all of the progressive peoples of the world. Not a surprise, but the first time it has been stated so clearly.

All of us, on the trip, I think share the same uneasiness about trying to decipher the truth and figuring out how best to read between the lines of many things said. We naturally can't tell how much repression there is, but there is something to be said for the fact that the city is filled with enough armed militia men and women for an uprising to occur if discontent were really widespread. I don't know where exactly the lack of freedom is. It certainly is frustrating to be given "the line" as often and as officially as we are, but we don't know if that is more a testimony to who we are and what we're expected to learn and do, or about the nature of the government. Some of each, undoubtedly, but still so hard to tell how it works. The easiest thing to describe is the seeming conformity of the population: very well ordered (also noticed that quality in the geographical layout of the countryside as we drove along); presence of official posters and propaganda all over; the loudspeakers which give the same news and music to everyone all over the city; clothing patterns. As well, the political slogans, the various organizational structures we've learned some about, are fairly traditional and very well-ordered lines.

For me (for us?) the problem will be to learn to communicate what we've seen to people in the U.S. without seeming brainwashed by DRV propaganda but by being able to give concrete evidence. We have little so far, only what we've been told about production figures, etc. It's true that just

---

[37] Pham Ngoc Thach, minister of health, and Pham Van Bach, head of the Supreme Court.

physical description of some things we've seen is key (Hanoi, bombing, especially along Route 1) but we haven't concrete evidence about proof of x bombs at y site on z day.

All of us must avoid doing what the pro-Soviet people did in the 1930s. How do we communicate a sense of the country, an acknowledgement of communism, our awareness of some of the restrictions and less attractive characteristics, with an insistence on the atrocities of the war. One way is to suggest that the LBJ presence is worse than any form of communism we've seen.[38] Another is to try to find independent ways of verifying some of the massive data we've been given—but how? (Some independent French and English journals, etc. and even stuff in the American press on the South.)

We've been talking about another whole problem, which is the question of who we are perceived to be. There is an incredible amount of formal exchanges and protocol, generally handled by Tom as the delegation head, and in almost every single situation we've had formal presentations and the same official line, over and over again. I felt my patience wearing thin once or twice. What we don't know is how much we're expected to do that or how much we can do to alter that pattern. We have a pretty good sense of some things we want to see and learn which does not include formal, hack presentations. It includes seeing, as it were, common people, and witnessing for ourselves samples of education, production, etc. in action. We've requested such things, but to no avail so far.

What is the Peace Committee's specific interest in having us? Do they primarily want us to go to places as part of the U.S. peace movement, describe our work with militancy, and, in general, serve as morale boosters? (Which is essentially what we've been doing.) If so, why didn't they have a more peace-movement group? How well do they understand us—do they know we're totally unrepresentative of the peace movement, except for Tom, and, oddly enough, Jock? Tom insists they know us well; he also says they want every bit of information about America they can get. I haven't seen evidence of this—they're not at all interested in the non–peace movement movement (understandably), and if they do understand who we are and how we can work most effectively, then they should be filling our time differently. On the other hand, perhaps they realize our very limited effectiveness and think either that we're more useful to them doing the "banquet circuit" here, or that we're not the people who can really make use of the information we

---

[38] Referring to the foreign policy of U.S. President Lyndon Johnson.

want (like Harrison Salisbury[39] would). The argument Nick [Egleson] made earlier was that they wanted friends of the Vietnamese in the U.S. Again, if that's true, they're not giving us enough concrete evidence. Though, on the other hand, with as little as they've given us, it's absolutely true that the trip has had a profound effect on all of us and what we will do. Ironically, it violates our own better sense of how to study a situation and what to learn from it. I would still like to pursue with them the question of how they see us. There is a bit of humor about the fact that all of us are probably being treated more royally here than we'll ever be again in our lives—another strange contradiction of the situation.

Final comment on all this: there is a problem of language. The "line" gets cranked out so regularly and predictably, and we're expected to respond in kind. Fortunately, Tom is talented at this and willing to do it. But I worry about using their language and saying things which I think are bullshit or empty rhetoric. I've tried hard to say nothing I wouldn't say at home, but the pressure is often on for Vivian or me to "say some words," and I shudder to hear what I sound like.

Trip to Nam Ha Province

First, morning spent in looking at some stores for gifts to purchase later. Busy busy day in the sky—a second of 7 air alerts. 2 early morning (7:30 and 8:00), one at 11:00 a.m., the next during lunch. The 5th at about 3:15 with very audible bombing ("prime time") and much greater show of caution on the part of the hotel staff in ushering us to the shelters. 6th a half-hour later and the final one almost immediately.

Much of the preceding (formal speeches, etc.) was prompted by the trip to the province. Easily the most exciting and worthwhile part was the actual traveling. Going south, on Route 1, in a caravan of 4 camouflaged jeeps, we saw continuous destruction: repeated efforts to bomb the road and the parallel-running railroad, villages on either side, individual large buildings—all ruined. Also many shelters being built along the road. As it grew dark the frequency of trucks passed—difficult to see the contents but some were road-repair brigades, others carried machinery. Many Rus-

---

[39] Harrison Salisbury was a reporter for the *New York Times* who traveled to Hanoi in December 1966 just after reports of the beginning of U.S. bombing of that city. Harrison E. Salisbury *Behind the Lines—Hanoi: December 23, 1966–January 7, 1967* (New York: Harper and Row, 1967).

sian trucks; much scattered machinery in protected boxes along the route. In some cases thatched huts concealing equipment. Crews repairing the railway. They seem prepared to jump in and repair things immediately. But what is evident is the repeatedness and thoroughness of the U.S. attacks, not their success in stopping transport and communication. Surprisingly, we saw power lines standing all over.

First stop, in total darkness, was the razed town of Phu Le, formerly a town of 7,000 but totally evacuated. The U.S. claimed this was a major railroad crossroads (there is a railroad) and therefore a supply center to be eliminated. We were greeted by the Director of the District Foreign Relations Committee (whatever that is; it was to appear again in Nam Ha) and administrative committee members. It was first bombed December 1966, and, most recently, 14 September 1967. An estimated 500 sorties have been flown, and it is completely leveled.

Arrived Nam Ha Province (who knows where?!) about 9:00, greeted by Le Vy, Pham Huong (Vice Chairman of Town and District Administrative Committees), and representatives of the labor youth, Central Committee of the Province (admitted openly), and Foreign Relations Section.

Usual formalities and a stony-faced lady spilled hot cafe-au-lait all over me. The building must've been of the French once and clearly is used for foreign visitors (of which they've had many)—mosquito netting bed, etc. At first, for the first time, I had wild dreams about where I was, about seeing bomb damage, and all in total darkness. Directly under our beds were cement shelters (the local folk had dirt trenches) and the hospitality was overwhelming.

The entire day was characterized by waiting and super-security. In the morning a few of us "broke discipline" and took a half-hour walk along the river, through the rice paddies, on the roads. While walking there was loud and not-very-distant bombing, which we later learned was in Nam Dinh. We saw smoke of anti-aircraft shells and of one missile. What struck us (then, and later in the day) was the lack of defense: no alerts, no radar, and probably very little actual defense. The countryside is protected by its own morale. The effect of the bombing was to delay our trip into the city: we talked and rested and ate and rested ("you're very tired") and talked hack talk and rested; were entertained by a local troupe, mostly from the textile factory, who sang the usual songs and didn't look very happy; were visited by a labor heroine; and finally got onto the road.

1st stop: on the road, was before a bridge when planes were heard overhead (now Friday, October 6th). Got to an evacuated part of the Nam

Dinh city hospital. Met head of that section and several other people. The hospital was destroyed in 4 bombings and is now in several evacuated sections which must be neat, light, and mobile. (Much training from French resistance is useful.)

Hospitals in general have 4 [sic] tasks: (1) curing patients; (2) education—hygiene; (3) training cadres; (4) research, which includes work on local medicine and herbs (traditional medicine), minimizing war effects, physiology of women and children; (5) will be preparation for peace.

Evacuation determined by military consultations, and patterns vary—are ready for the "long march." Cardinal principles: no concentrations of technical equipment; mobility. We saw part of an ingenious building: collapsible building with thatched cover over iron set on cement base (which are built all over in preparation for transfers); operating lights provided by bicycle whose wheels are connected to a generator; sunken operating tables; mobile oxygen pumps. Also the unpleasant experience of seeing patients: 2 school kids, 2 workers. This part of the routine makes me shudder—I really resent it.

Then to Nam Dinh. First air attacks 28 June 1965, and since then 200 attacks on the inner and outer city, in all weather at all times of day. We saw:

(1) Phò Hang Thao: first bombed 14 April 1966, 6:30 a.m. Many children killed, 800 families were made homeless. Monument has been built in the street, which suggests no reason for having been bombed.

(2) Phô Hoang Van Thu: bombed 18 May 1966 at noon. By far the most extensive damage I've seen inside a city. One thousand families made homeless. Attacked again 30 June 1966 and 25 December 1966. Ironically, while walking in the ruins we came across a Catholic Church and heard the Mass. Also monument at this site. Also damaged by bombings: 25 May 1967, a special section of the city for repatriates from Thailand, other countries; 22 June 1967, much of the harvest, from heavy bombing.

Targets have included rice fields, residential areas, schools (inner city), pagodas, hospitals, even a cemetery, and the dikes (7 times). All 16 district capitals in the province have been attacked, there has been massive evacuation—the city is really empty. But, we were informed, production goes on (and improves), and schools and medical facilities continue their work. Textiles was the major industry of the city.

One interesting characteristic of the man (Le Vy) who escorted us all day was that he was much more the party hack than others we've met. But he was also much more direct in his language—reference to Workers' Party, to socialism; and at one point he asserted that there is no right to argue that people in one part of a country shouldn't help their fellow countrymen in another part.

One woman, a teacher, during the afternoon, read us a poem by her 25-year-old brother killed April 1966 at Hang Thao Street. A rough interpretation (written March 1966, about youth):

> Youth is the core of life, and he who has experienced it loves it.
> When you stretch your arms to fly from dark to bright, and not from
>   morning to evening,
> What shall you do when you're young?
>
> Don't ask many questions—
> When little brother killed day and night by U.S. pirates,
> When our heart is chilled by cold wind,
>   How can we sleep and eat easily?
>
> If in our youth we hold a plow or iron hammer or capture pilots,
>   that is heroism.
> But if a bullet comes from one angle of our eyes aiming at the enemy,
>   this is the highest act.
>
> Youth doesn't mean marching behind mothers.
> It means to fly to faraway regions.
> Don't behave like tigers frightened of sharp bamboo, or like bears
>   with thick hair who sleep all winter.
> Don't be satisfied like a white dove which looks at life naïvely or
>   only to take its daily grain.
>
> The strength of the "badame" tree doesn't come from its green
>   leaves, but from its sap.
> A man is strong not from his two rosy cheeks, but from his brain,
>   heartbeat, and calloused hands.
>
> Our youth is like a bird—but don't compare them to an owl.
> Compare youth to a flower, but not to an odorless flower.
> Compare youth to a tree, but not an ordinary tree.
> Youth is like the core of life, and must grow into the finest.

Also in Nam Dinh—in the dark—we finally saw an underground factory: several units of a welding shop (with lathes and polishing machines), with the machinery sunken. Also underground workers' rest places. And adjacent, next to an open field (playground?) were militia women with light caliber guns and a group of young women of the self-defense unit preparing for a training session. Last stop was at a school, for young girls, open air roof, guns on the wall, on the street which had been bombed that morning (and 1 person killed). Perfectly prepared for us, the lesson of the day was about Norman Morrison,[40] one of the more obvious set-ups we've encountered. Nevertheless, seeing the reality of the school was exciting, the factory even more so.

Hanoi, Day 9: Saturday, October 7. Air alerts; mayor of Hanoi; evening, Women's Union and East German film

Saturday, 7th October 1967

Been here one week. Arrived back from the province, wearily at 2:00 a.m. Woken by alert at 7:45 which lasted 45 minutes. Record length, and we heard a lot of bombing. Another alert woke us at 11:15 a.m., and an alert (audible bombing) at 1:00 p.m.

Main event of the day was seeing the mayor of Hanoi, a very delightful, thorough, charming, and methodical man. Probably quite powerful—he has been mayor since 1945 and he and Ho Chi Minh are the only 2 Deputies from Hanoi to the National Assembly dating back to 1945. He is 55 years old, name is Tran Duy Hung. We asked a whole series of questions about city administration, etc., and his response was a careful summary (detailed) of a civics textbook. Excellently presented, with proper acknowledgement of the "line"—we should have known it all beforehand and been ready to pose much more specific questions. He was quite candid, and Oanh's translation was good. Still have not pieced together entirely the structure, but here are some of the main features.

First, anyone over 18 can vote. (Oanh said "forced" but he may have

---

[40] Norman Morrison was a thirty-two-year-old Quaker who burned himself to death in front of the Pentagon on November 2, 1965, to protest the war in Vietnam. Following the example of Vietnamese Buddhists who had performed the same gruesome act in protest of Diem's policies in South Vietnam, Morrison used self-immolation as an expression of his antiwar beliefs. DeBenedetti, *An American Ordeal*, 129–30.

Tran Duy Hung, mayor of Hanoi, with Carol McEldowney (LEFT) *and Vivian Rothstein, October 7 (photographer unknown).*

not intended that.) The city is divided into electoral districts (how many?). The collectives of each district, which include factories, schools, theaters, housewives, street quarter units, can propose 3 candidates. Person from each collective brings suggestions to consultative meeting which evaluates candidates from all districts. Also can be free candidates (who are successful workers, and well liked in their street quarters), but in the last election in 1964—160 collective candidates were proposed and 12 free candidates (who received a small percent of the vote). 135 candidates were chosen from the city to form the Hanoi People's Council [HPC].

Therefore, step (1): district picks candidates, from collectives, with aid of consultative meeting. Step (2): districts send their 3 names to a committee of the Fatherland Front[41] composed of representatives from each mass organization (women, unions, religious, Chinese, non-affiliates (street quarters), peasants, etc.). Step (3): names returned by Fatherland Front to the base. 2 weeks pre-election the candidates appear before the Electorate to "prove what they've done," and the week before Elections there is discussion.

---

[41] The Fatherland Front was established in 1953 in Hanoi. Though intended to represent all of Vietnam, in the South it was replaced by the National Liberation Front (NLF) after 1960.

Hanoi People's Council is elected every 3 years. Current composition: 33% workers; 11% peasants; 21% intellectuals, medical people, artists, teachers; 4% religious people: (21% are women); army representative; some are representatives of cadres of mass organizations and 2 members of the National Bourgeoisie (1 big capitalist!).

The mayor is responsible for city life in general. But Hanoi is the capital and has present many things on a national level. The Mayor also administers these and here is directly related (responsible) to the National Assembly, as well as working with the Prime Minister and President. This includes administration of large industries, including state-owned (which are these?), "social bodies" such as universities. In general he is to "safeguard common property."

National Assembly is administered by a standing committee—no more information on this now.

Concept of a collective is misty. Is this primarily a party cell? Collectives suggest candidates for the HPC, and they are responsible to the HPC and administrative committee on city management questions.

(Cadre defined by Oanh as full-time or half-time (other half for production) for permanent organization or administrative committee. Organizational workers? Administrative cadres must work ⅓ time at their base.)

Dispersal (preferred to evacuation)

From 1954 on, the city grew rapidly and became a city of production rather than consumption. In 1954, population was 249,000; grew to 600,000 inner city and 550,000 outskirts by 1964. Principles:

1. Best protection provided by dispersal, in this order: (a) school age children; non-weaning children, old people. Neighboring provinces were prepared over a long time to receive Hanoi's children. The administration was/is responsible for transportation, food supply, and education of these children. Living conditions have been tightened, but progress is being made. Trade Unions, for example, had an "assistance program" to raise provisions for dispersed families. To date 250,000 children have been dispersed. And school enrollment has been increased. From 1966 to 1967, increase was 17%, and 1967 to 1968, increase was 11% (1st, 2nd, and 3rd grades.) (b) Production base also has been dispersed. Transportation was very difficult at first, but has been stabilized. Still a problem at times, but positive effect has increased understanding and alliance between dispersed workers and the peasants of the countryside.

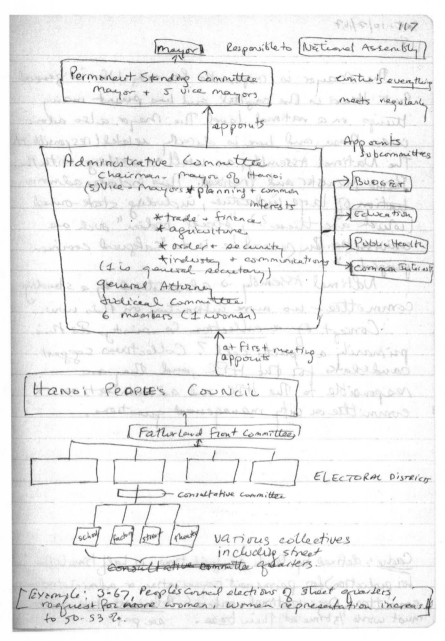

Chart of Hanoi's governmental structure.

2. Adequate shelter and normal education, production and life for those remaining in Hanoi. Necessary production units remain in the city. People in the streets are protected, but also prepared for dispersal, which is district committee responsibility.

Within Hanoi, supply and service patterns have changed dramatically: work is now done in small sectors. In some areas, personnel has increased (e.g., shops, up ⅓) because of the new need for mobile units; public health programs have scattered and need more people. Same for teachers. But the amount of work required of people has increased even more (e.g., teachers must now help manage the lives of the dispersed children).

Plans for city, and brief history since 1954: In 1954, after Hanoi was liberated (10 October 1954) there were serious problems of prostitution, unemployment, diseases, garbage, begging, gambling houses, opium, etc.[42] And the city was <u>unproductive</u>. Were many French imported goods. Illiteracy was 95%; were only 48,000 schoolchildren, and 5,000 workers.

1st job was to assure "order, security, and production." 1954–56 was period of "Restoration of Hanoi economy": railroads, new small factories built, new sections of city. By 1956 "socialist transformation of various economic components" progressed, and more factories built. (Land reform on city outskirts occurred 1955.) Hanoi was a city of production by 1958. 1960 first 5-year plan began to "Increase Production to Increase Basic Part of the Population—i.e., Workers," to make Hanoi an industrial center, and develop its education and culture. <u>Principle</u>: industrial economic basis. But also broaden streets, build parks, etc.

Hanoi has become a socialist city since 1960. Much help provided from "brother socialist countries." The spirit of workers and peasants has been very important. Now, rank and file (workers, technicians) are 29% of population. (Many are advanced educationally through night school.) Many labor heroes were formerly poor people. (Those workers now in the city must protect their production, and they are prepared in self-defense.)

Future plans: have learned that each city has its own demands and spirit, in line with the national spirit. The subcommittee of the HPC on Planning and <u>Reconstruction</u> continues its work. There will be some transformation of the city whether or not it is destroyed. Areas have been bombed (including homes near the dikes in December 1966 and May 1967) and living

---

[42] French control of Vietnam ended in 1954 after the French were defeated at Dien Bien Phu by the Viet Minh.

conditions may be tighter. But there will be a post-war reconstruction plan, when peace comes.

Saturday evening

Meeting with Women's Union—(Ha Giang).[43] Vivian and I prepared a list of questions, most of which didn't really get answered. The three women were older than we hoped for, and obviously used to foreigners. They described the status of women before the Revolution, and since.

During feudalism (and up to August 1945) women were slaves of slaves. They had no rights (except a few rich city women), no good job positions, were highly illiterate. Factories discriminated in pay (½ that of men), managers beat women. Peasant life had long hard hours.

The new constitution guaranteed equality for men and women in work and pay, and right of election. Premier Pham Van Dong heads the committee for defense of women and children, which has power to resolve various problems, and deals with things such as social and labor insurance. Briefly, political life: National Assembly, 16% women (66). Women are vice-chairmen of some National Assembly standing committees. Vice-Ministers of Light Industry, Public Health, Labor (2) are women. No chairmen, note! 50% people's councils on district and village levels are women. Women usually vice-chairmen of administrative committees of districts and communes, and of agricultural cooperatives.

My own feeling is that this is a lot of bullshit—in almost every situation we've encountered men clearly take the lead, and there is a kind of servility, and subservience of women, especially in villages we've seen. The statistics don't give me a sense of equality.

Employment: women are taking work suitable to their capacity and physical conditions. Education and public health fields likely to be 70–80% women. Many women in light industry. Childcare is very important, and programs are provided for all employed mothers (nurseries, etc.).

Pregnancy and birth control: a major principle is protection of women's health, before and after pregnancy, and after work as well. Many local level health centers concentrate on maternal health. Women must be enabled to work and study, and to have good childcare. And they must be able to help defend their country. Birth control is widespread—accepted—and

---

[43] See note 10.

taught to men as well. Some policies of the government are contrary to religious teachings, such as birth control. But motto adopted by Catholics has been—when in life, follow the DRV (which provides adequate food, clothing, and shelter), and when in death, follow god and the church. (The Women's Union was surprisingly frank on this point.)

Know about the Women's Union (mass organization) and its "3 Responsibilities" movement from the Bratislava meeting (see previous notes) but still don't have a sense of where women are in the society. Especially young women and city women, who undoubtedly will not go back peacefully to being housewives after the war. Am very interested to see what kinds of social patterns emerge. Women cutting their hair is one concrete example of breaking ties with traditional culture. And there may be more professional women. Much culture seems to depend on the femininity of women, which does seem to be maintained—but the effects of women in industry, of women giving orders, of small families, is bound to be great. . . .

Late evening. Saw an East German (GDR) film called Mother in Silence, about the German Communist Party under the Nazis (1934?). The German was blocked out, with a Vietnamese soundtrack over it. The film was terrible: painted the CP as bunch of bourgeoisie, characterized by an old mother, and was fairly kind to the Nazis. Surrealistic. Especially to stand up at the end and find myself surrounded by Vietnamese!

Hanoi, Day 10: Sunday, October 8. Museum of Arts and Handicrafts; Nguyen Minh Vy of Thong Nhat; evening, meeting to prepare for visit with captured pilots

Sunday, 8 October 1967

First night alert, at 2:30 a.m. Hotel lights were quickly turned off (scary for a minute) and we heard a lot of bombings.

7:45: to Bao Tang My Thuat My Nghe (Museum of Arts and Handicrafts). First opened June 1966, and partly evacuated, for the protection of valuable items (which are now only viewable as copies). (2nd air alert.) Building was formerly a French boarding school, and it was a huge, graceless construction—that French-style architecture is all over Hanoi and is very unattractive. The task of the museum is to satisfy the people's cultural needs. There are 2 main sections: classic arts (Stone Age till nineteenth century—strange!); and <u>contemporary</u> (nineteenth century to present day). Also, a special section on folk arts and handicrafts and arts of ethnic minorities of the northwest and northeast.

The museum is supposed to be national, but in fact is really a museum of the North. Some highlights:

- Bronze age display, especially huge drums depicting culture, weapons, of the time, 2,000 years ago.
- 11th–12th century stone age, very imposing.
- <u>Buddhism</u>: many huge old idols, similar to what we saw at Angkor Wat. Seeing these really gives me a sense of the domination and extent of the influence of this tradition—how it must saturate the history—and how unresponsive to Christianity it must be. Particularly struck by a 1656 statue of Buddha with 1,000 eyes (and hands) over 4 oceans (which ones, I wonder).
- Ethnic (old and current) arts are a brilliant art of color, so lovely, a little like early Mexican life. The liveliness and persuasiveness of the culture really comes through—so hard to imagine another (western) culture successfully being imposed on it. Wonderful handicrafts, too.
- Various drawings of old life—almost like an Eastern Brueghel, but not quite so obscene. But real picture-like drawings.
- Influence of oriental mythology apparent in dragons and fishes. Wish I knew more. . . .
- Oriental art <u>is</u> different. Partly, different substances (silk, lacquer, oyster shell)! But content as well. I like much of it but really don't understand it very well. Would like to see a lot more.
- <u>Contemporary</u>—mostly paintings from 1945 to the present. Some good, some pretty hack social commentary. Some very good political sketches (a little reminiscent of Daumier).[44] But I've seen too much of this already to be very inspired by it.

Vuong Nho Chiem, an art critic and sculptor, hosted us at the Museum—he's probably one of the most unusual people I've met. Very much a poetic personality; and style. Talked about the need for culture to be preserved, of children's need for culture. And he spoke very little of the war and U.S. aggression. When he did, it was in terms of its effect on culture. He was sincere, and likeable, and not at all hackneyed in his language. On the contrary, his love of culture, art, etc. really showed. He was also one of the few

---

[44] Honoré Daumier was a nineteenth-century French caricaturist and painter.

people to watch and see what in the museum interested <u>us</u> and then explain, instead of picking things for us.

A very valuable experience. Spoke of how he is here today . . . and tomorrow might be gone.

3 p.m. alert.

Visit with Nguyen Minh <u>Vy</u>. He is slowly being revealed to us as much more important than we suspected. He is Director of the paper <u>Thong Nhat</u>, a member of the National Assembly, Secretary of the Peace Committee, and head of the Department of Information. (Director: general line policy; Editor-in-Chief: layout, specific articles, deadlines; Editorial Board: secretary (Chief Editor and 3 members.)

We spoke to him first in his role as <u>Thong Nhat (Reunification)</u> Director. Also met Mr. Phung, international part of paper, and Mr. Sac, Secretary of the Editorial Board. <u>Thong Nhat</u> was established in 1957 by regrouped Southerners in the North, when reunification elections didn't occur. Began as weekly and now is twice a week. Its goal is its title—educate people in the struggle for reunity. Main part of the paper is for news and specific stories about South Vietnam. Second part is international support of the struggle (wide range of commentary from U.S. peace movement to U.S. Senate speeches to <u>National Guardian</u> articles). Third part: Northern support of the struggle in the South (for example, through "brother province" program in which a province in the North works with a Southern province by using its victories for names, and material support will be provided after liberation. Example: Hanoi–Saigon; Nam Ha–My Tho. Also, paper has articles from the South (including poets, etc.). It reaches people in Cambodia <u>and</u> the South, has a relationship with Giai Phong Press, with other DRV papers, and with various foreign papers of socialist countries (e.g., <u>Wochen-Post</u> in East Germany).

<u>Vy</u> and the Department (Ministry?) of Information: job is to organize people, to "agitate population in production and fighting," to read papers, listen to radio, etc. The department is <u>not</u> connected with newspapers or radios. It <u>does</u> have responsibility for

• Hanoi Information Center
• Billboards all over the city
• My Bai scoreboards: these are organized by "street quarters"—each has an "information team" (volunteer) which announces plane scores, as well as production plans, and explains important news to people on house-to-house basis. Most of this work is done by youth, and information also carried to factories, cooperatives, etc.
• Loudspeakers, for information (also used by military for air alerts)

In general, base in universities and schools is very important. Teachers are information agents: daily they announce important news which children carry to their parents.

(Meeting is planned with the journalists—hopefully will learn more about the press. Do know that <u>Nhan Dan</u> is <u>major</u> paper, and it is daily paper of the Workers' Party.)

<u>Evening</u>: preparations to see captured American pilots by visiting with Mr. Bai, officer in charge, and 4 others, 3 of whom we discovered were translators for the VPA (one, Nguyen Van Vy, friend of Carol Brightman).

Whole situation was rather eerie. Drove into a place guarded with top security. Smelled of richly perfumed flowers, music was in the background, and everyone was in uniform. Vietnam or the U.S.—a uniform is a uniform and it made me shudder—really uneasily. Conversation was stiff for a long formal time—and I got a sense of how hard it may be to actually speak with the pilots. They informed us of their humanitarian treatment of the pilots (who do not deserve POW status); even those punished for breaking camp rules are not physically punished. We discussed the problem of "brainwashing." They assured us it hadn't occurred. All very strange. They said some pilots have been taken to actually see bomb damage or to meet injured children. They of course are quite anxious to know the effect of our seeing them on Americans. Their task, they say, is to make them better American citizens when they return home. Mr. Bai warned us of 2 problems: to know when to speak of their consciousness of what they've done, and how to avoid doing or saying things that will make it hard for them to repatriate. (Interpretation really broke down here, so it may be all wrong.) But they are concerned with the psychology of the pilots. Special requests were made (by Jock) to visit sick pilots and (by Bob) to tape an interview. Supposed to have another session with Bai to approve this stuff.

Also saw a short film of the prisoners with special treats on Christmas Day. VPA itself isn't sure how it will use the film—no soundtrack yet. A very strange experience—seeing the pilots will be stranger.

Monday night we got a slightly more digestible view of the Army—saw a rehearsal of their entertainment team preparing for the 10-10-Hanoi liberation celebration.[45] Some really good dancing, and some not-so-good singing. And some excellent music (monochord, bamboo flute). Some people in

---

[45] Refers to the liberation of Vietnam on October 10, 1954.

Army uniform, some in native costumes. The graceful art of the women's hands in the dancing is absolutely beautiful. I felt a little more understanding of the VPA after this—although admittedly my patience was wearing thin with the absolutely similar content of each number (all anti-war, but much of it hackneyed-sounding).

Hanoi and Dan Phuong, Day 11: Monday, October 9.
Trip to Dan Phuong Cooperative

Monday, 9 October 1967

By 10:00 a.m. we had put in a 6-hr day. The feature of the day was a trip to Dan Phuong Cooperative, in the district and province of the same name, some 22 km. from Hanoi. (Means Red Phoenix.) It appears to be a model cooperative, having acquired several awards since it was established. In 1945 the area was liberated; it was reoccupied by the French in 1947 and held by them until 1953. During this time there was 90% illiteracy, no maternity houses, only 1 school, and ⅔ of the land was owned by the landlords.

Now, the cooperative encompasses the entire village. (Often a village will have several cooperatives.) There are 1,000 households and 5,000 people in the village. Anyone who wants can join the cooperative. Those who don't can live as private citizens (this is but 2% now) but the village administrative committee "encourages" membership!

Our "official meeting" was held in a large old French building, easily the largest around. Our escort was Mr. Thach, Cooperative Director. Also present were the local head of the Fatherland Front Committee, the Women's Union, Youth Organization, old age representative. The cooperative is governed by a 19-member <u>Managing Board</u>, elected by a congress of cooperative members. Members include responsibilities for planning and production (5); finance and distribution (1); science and technique (1); animal breeding (1); fighting and security (1); culture and life (1); heads of production teams (9?). The cooperative is concerned with <u>production</u>. The village has its own People's Council and Administrative Committee, which deals with other aspects of life.

The cooperative plan is based on the recommended state plan for districts and villages, etc., but the cooperative members approve it (the language one begins to use is remarkable—I have been careful in trying to use their language without always implying my judgment of what that really means. For example, it was rather clear that the cooperative plan is the state plan, but it is important to acknowledge that the cooperative decides).

There are 2 methods of distribution:

1. food (rice, potatoes, some supplementary food) is distributed: 75% to cooperative members; 10% for reproduction; and 15% for state. Within the cooperative distribution is according to age.
2. money, income from production sales: 50% cooperative members; 30% expenses; 10% reproduction; 10% state.

Within the cooperative, the average labor days (8 hours) a year is two hundred. Actual labor days vary, 150 to 250 days. And work is distributed according to skills and health of members. (Different for old people and children.) Individuals receive money according to the labor days they have worked. At the end of the year, the portions for the state and reproduction are subtracted, and the rest is for cooperative members. Individuals can also maintain private gardens, fish ponds, etc. for their own consumption, but they must meet cooperative production standards overall.

The cooperative has 350 arable hectares, or 1 hectare per 12 people. The "socialist rice field" has been achieved! This year rice yield increased from 4 to 7 tons per hectare. Per capita production was 200 kilograms; 200 tons went to the state. Also—a major success: pig production (58 tons produced). (Also very deceptive—they looked like terrible pigs, mostly fat—we don't know their feed, relative meat/fat yield, their use (meat or breeding), so all these figures are almost impossible to analyze without some expertise.) Did learn that they have 5 pig breeding units, and cows are used for agriculture.

We did see some interesting things there: a school, thatched hut, kids immediately arose with military discipline. About 35 kids in the class, with 9 girls all at the back. 11–12-year-olds, 4th grade equivalent, with 8 kids from Hanoi. The school is surrounded by dirt walls and shelters, all the kids carry pellet hats, and some had first-aid kits. The whole village has over 20 such schools, with 1–2 classes each. (Their schooling has 3 levels, each with about 4 years, roughly equivalent to our primary, junior high, senior high.) Couldn't tell if the kids were prepared for us—but we came on them suddenly and hadn't even realized the presence of the school.

Walked around the cooperative some and had many different reactions. The fields themselves looked beautiful: rice, fertilizer. Also saw lots of lotus, water lilies, and fish. On the other hand we didn't see the fruit orchards, banana trees, or animals. In fact, we didn't see any field where people were working, something which continually befuddles me—why the reluctance to let us see people at work? It would be so much more real to see that. Also saw the improving irrigation system, as well as a sample of the 20,000 pine trees which have been recently planted as windbreakers. Strange indeed to look down a row of pine trees on a rise separating rice paddies and see a dirt shelter under each. Also growing 18,000 trees of a different variety which will provide enough wood for houses in 5 years.

Walking into the village was a different experience. Many people, but many old people (some probably dispersed from Hanoi) and lots of little kids which made me wonder more about the schools and why they weren't in them. The homes varied—some brick, some traditionally thatched mud huts. Very crowded, but frequently with patios. Most striking is the age—saw several yards with dated gates (1959, 1960) which looked much more ancient (more like 1910). If those dates are accurate, it makes me appreciate how much newer Hanoi actually is: the stucco or paint over wood or bamboo weathers very rapidly. And much of the housing in Hanoi easily looks 30 years older than its actual age. Common pattern in the village looked to be a common patio (with huge cooking pots), probably dirt floors in the huts. But we couldn't really see inside. Poverty seemed abundant—yet that, too, may be a deception. It impresses me over and over again that my view of life from such an industrialized country as the U.S. gives me no experience to look and evaluate rural economy. No standards, no methods to judge what is well-off, what is poor, nor do I know what it is all relative to—lots of living conditions in the city look ghetto-like in the age, dinginess, crowdedness, etc. But, on the other hand, it looks clean, and so different that comparisons have little value. What that means is that a Westerner, to evaluate the economic prosperousness of citizens, must either rely on statistics, or be here a long time and really learn the conditions. It is sad but true that we must do the former, if either, and be careful not to make judgments based on our own western city standards and experiences. I wish it were different—I also wish I could stick my nose into more people's houses. (Tám says his family—wife and 2 kids—have a house with 1 room up and 1 room down—which I saw from the outside. Looked small by our standards but is probably fairly "middle class" here.)

Back to the village: walked around, saw old village common house and culture house, now both used for rice storage, facing each other across a broad patio, with a loudspeaker near by. Also saw delightfully funny political cartoons drawn on building walls. I did come away with a sense of community—closeness?—within the village. I'm sorry I couldn't get more of a sense of how the village itself is organized geographically. I suspect it is rather regular, but it was hard to depict this walking around.

During the morning the U.S. planes keep the village busy. Between 7:30 and 8:00 a.m., while in the reception room, we constantly heard planes and distant bombing and kept going back and forth into the shelters, though nothing was really close. Yet it became a pain—easy to see how people are used to it and expect it, yet without question it interrupts their lives, all the time. (In Hanoi we were out shopping—4:00 p.m. Monday—and there was an alert. First time we've been in the street rather than a building when that happened, and people really do move rapidly to the shelters, when the alert sounds, after being warned by the loudspeakers that the plane is 70km., 60 km., and finally 50 km. from the city.)

When we first entered the cooperative, we spoke a while with one of the militia girls of the self-defense squad. The squad is composed mostly of 18–23-year-old girls (must be natives of the village). They are on duty for 10 days to 1 month, then rotate with 2 other squads. They are on duty 1 hour, off the next. They were using Chinese machine guns with a 3,000 meter range (c. 2 miles), but usually used at 1,800 meters (c. 1 mile) and their main job is to scare the planes up high enough for the missiles (anti-aircraft?) to get them. The alert system uses gongs and seems tightly organized. The girl I spoke to (23 years) was a tough but young looking girl. They're so young, so little—so determined. This girl had a kind of determination (and not much use for foreigners) which I really liked—almost found myself having nothing meaningful to say to her.

Later met a militia girl (19 years) who had helped shoot down a U.S. plane 22 April 1966. She told the story of 3 units of 4 jets each approaching, the last unit diving low, and one plane of that group was hit.

Also met a 14-year-old boy who was badly burned in the winter of 1964. Has been in the hospital 3 years and therefore only in the 5th year now instead of the 8th. He has evacuated to the village and is "normal" again, in spite of enormous scars across his entire back.

As usual, of the most interesting features of the cooperative was the traveling to and from. Oanh had said that not only must we have military approval for trips, but no foreigners are allowed to see troops or supply conveys on the road, and often trips are rerouted or the military reroutes their plans. This explains even more the huge problems involved in traveling. Therefore, it was much to our surprise, on the way back, to see the road literally lined, for one long stretch, with all kinds of equipment: Czech trucks, huge mobile generators (Russian), and what were obviously missile carriers (all empty, we think). Why we were allowed to see it I'm not sure. Its appearance caused some speculation about bombing: our guess was that it would be nearly impossible for a plane to get in low enough to pick a target of one truck—would be shot up before that. And even if a plane came tearing down the road, it would be picked off. I'm beginning to learn some of the language, but am still pretty naïve about a lot of technical language—strafing, bombing, which planes do what and at which levels. (Am learning it, though.)

Also on the road I saw, as I've seen on every road, many bricks. They are easily manufactured in almost every village—rapidly. Cement production is also being dispersed. (Air alert around 4:00 p.m. while shopping. We went to the shelters by the lake, so did everyone else.)

Hanoi, Day 12: Tuesday, October 10. Committee on
Cultural Relations with Foreign Countries

Tuesday, 10 October 1967

Afternoon: meeting with Committee on Cultural Relations with Foreign Countries (with Pham Hong, Vice Secretary General of Peace Committee; Mrs. Cuc, distribution; and several others). This committee is responsible to the Council of Ministers (like a Cabinet).

It relates to all countries:
• socialist: regular exchanges on an annual plan, including cultural, technical, and scientific
• nationalist countries
• capitalist—occasional exchange of cultural delegations and publications

Committee also is responsible for propaganda work for foreign countries. This includes: Foreign Language Publishing House, Vietnam Courier (English, French), Vietnam Magazine (French, English, Chinese, Russian, Spanish, Vietnamese). Nothing has yet been produced specially for Americans or GIs.

We began to touch on the propaganda and exchange question. They regularly receive National Guardian; rarely get Liberation; sometimes see English materials of other offices. They want contact with booksellers, more English material, and help in improving their English (much of which is rather poor).

What kind of propaganda network will get established is debatable. Many people in the U.S. and at the Bratislava meeting made all sorts of promises, but a good job really requires coordination. This is one of the things I must think about further, and try to talk about with people here before we split.

The chance has come up for all of us to make a tape for the NLF to use for GIs. Only Tom is definite. I have mixed feelings about whether we here should do that, though I'm fairly certain it would be worthwhile for some tapes to be made in the U.S. and sent over. (We will have a chance to evaluate an English NLF broadcast.)

Also saw, with Committee on Cultural Relations, a beautiful film on dances (traditional, ethnic, province, etc.) followed by the very effective film on Nguyen Van Troi—extremely emotional and excellent (especially since I had just read the book). I think it would be a good film to bring home. It's true some people may have questions about celebrating someone who tried to kill McNamara, but in general I think the film can only have a positive effect (presented as an example of a Vietnamese legend in the revolutionary struggle). The torture scenes and solidarity jail scenes are also very powerful. Film was translated for Vivian and me by a lovely young woman who works for the Courier, Ho Kim Thu. (Also—film showed the inside of a home of a Vietnamese couple—how average I don't know—but interesting.)

Evening: for some reason the meeting with the pilots is delayed and may not occur. No further information on this. Fortunately dinner was late and with a long walk afterwards, time passed. We have so much time on our hands, and I find it really difficult to write/think here, in the hotel situation and all that. Haven't written about that: French-style mosquito-netting around beds; waiters here who undoubtedly served the French and bow and cajole all the time; massive amounts of (often poor) French-style cooking—3 meals daily and an attempt to stuff us at each; the numerous foreign journalists who seem to sit at the bar all day, especially the loud Russians. Egads what a place the Unity Hotel (Thong Nhat) is! It turns out that if we tally our total work hours spent, they would easily be crammed into one week.

Some insightful miscellaneous conversation with Hieu, whom I'm growing extremely fond of, a very warm affectionate person, patient, and interested in us.

- Cadres: originally refers to workers of the revolutionary party when still clandestine. Then continued to be used for all government workers. Now used as well for workers for mass organizations. Main element is work at the base, with the masses—mobilization work.

"Organizer" is used for something specific, example, organize for meeting (Cân bó).

- Delightful insights into how the population is mobilized. Always a general statement about mobilizing, educating the masses, and <u>not</u> forcing them. Must maintain the "mass line." Example Hieu used: peasants especially are conservative and resist new methods. So sometimes the state official goes to the farm with new seed, for example; peasants try it reluctantly; a film is then made and soon after shown to the peasants who are then won over!

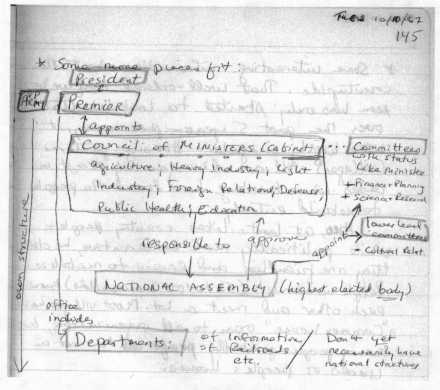

Chart of North Vietnam's governmental administrative structure.

Locally, administrative committees exist down to village level. Each has committees on production and inner affairs. And at the province level may have foreign relations, which is responsible to <u>its</u> administrative council.

Some interesting information about the countryside. That well-ordered turf we've seen has only started to look like that over the past 5 years—

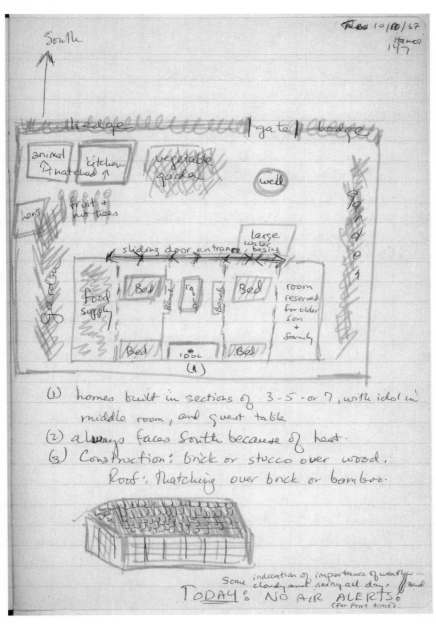

Sketch of village layout.

Hanoi, September 29–October 17, 1967   81

previously, it was highly irregular. Housing patterns (villages) still are disorganized except in cases where bombing has forced the people to rebuild entirely.

Hieu, at least, likes country people—while politically more conservative, he claims they are friendlier and easier to mobilize. People in hamlets (5 to 100 households) know each other and meet a lot. Most villages have a "Common House" open to all organizations, but many people probably prefer to meet in yards or people's homes.

Rebuilding villages (housing) is not a high priority now, relative to other things; in the countryside the emphasis is on production.

A word (Oanh's) on guerilla fighting principles, or "why the U.S. cannot win": (1) guerilla must know the land; and (2) must be close to the people.

Today: some indication of the importance of weather, cloudy and rainy all day and NO AIR ALERTS! (for first time).

Hanoi, Day 13: Wednesday, October 11. Viewing of Dien Bien Phu *at the Museum of the Revolution; Mr. Ky and the Journalists' Association; evening, meeting with intellectuals*

Wednesday, 11 October 1967

Delightful experience early this morning: it was pouring rain, and I put on a borrowed raincoat and a Vietnamese conical hat and went to take a walk. Saw a lot: little workshops (tailor, instruments), people going on in spite of the rain (a sense of life during the rainy season). Ventured into one store and asked them for chopsticks (dua). An old lady took me by the hand down the block to ask where to get them. Failure. But for a brief moment I sat inside a house with two chattering oldish women and it really was a rare experience of being with absolutely ordinary people. Then back to the store, and communication in pidgin French with a guy there. Finally, the woman left, but to quickly reappear with 3 pairs of her own chopsticks. After a bit of wrangling, she finally took some money (1 Đ)[46] and I explained to the guy in French who I was (much surprise and a fair amount of warmth), and left. A rare treat to have used chopsticks from an old Vietnamese lady.

Then to the Museum of the Revolution to see the film on Dien Bien Phu.

---

[46] Vietnamese currency is the dong (Đ).

We were greeted by an extremely warm and cheerful group of directors, critics, cameramen, etc., including Quynh who was the man responsible for film development at Dien Bien Phu (now a director of documentaries), Bach Tiet (Director, feature films). Nguyen Thu, an incredibly beautiful guy with high cheekbones and a warm, gentle, and soulful smile, and a DBP original introduced it.

Made in 1954 with enormous technical difficulties: started with 2 cameras and operators; the 3rd camera was U.S. and captured from the French. Film was scarce and provided by the people; the developer was wooden and hand-cranked. The principle, however, was great mobility of the operators. Thu humorously concluded that all the original equipment is now museum encased except the operators!

We saw a version redone in 1964, but using all the original footage.

The film itself was inspiring. I came away thinking of the very different (and complete) role the Army plays in this society—so entirely different from any concepts within the American movement. There, at DBP, and now, the Army is a total structure, with active people's support. And very important. Military achievement is greatly valued in a society that has been at war 20 years. In the U.S. there is absolutely no reality to the idea of an Army being with the people (or their leader). Also got a feeling for the different attitude towards death and life which pervades the society and is both strange to us and difficult to understand. The Vietnamese idolization of Morrison is an example. Yet he's barely known in the U.S. movement and most people don't understand why he burned himself to death (I'm not, except that it expressed an understanding of the Vietnamese way . . .).

Film also very good in its footage of trench-building. Gave me a better sense of guerilla fighting. For example, in the final stages, the Vietnamese succeeded in getting a lot of French supplies that were dropped.

Miscellaneous note: cannons apparently are called "elephants" and the "Elephant Song" we've heard several times is, in fact, about weapons!

Afternoon—one of the funniest events yet. Met with Mr. Ky of the Journalists' Association. We were there nearly 3 hours—the first 1½ hours was unbearable for me because Ky came across with the most blatant line yet on propaganda. But the next 1½ hours, he began telling story after story and it was warm, folksy, and very informative as well. Everything was in story form (he talked endlessly!) and even invented "an old Vietnamese saying" especially for us (about friends who come 10,000 miles . . .).

The "humor" was much of his description of the newspapers and "truth control," etc. First, the Journalists' Association is a mass organization, with about 2,000 journalists. There are journalists of 3 types of journals: (1) mass organizations, published in Hanoi, 30; (2) provinces (and military zones), 40; and (3) science and technology branches, 370. The Association is more than a trade union. Its purposes:

1. professional exchanges of experiences
2. unify and mobilize journalists
3. problems of working conditions of journalists

The purposes of journalism are:

1. serve Revolution and fatherland
2. present the truth
3. have a "mass character"

Journalists are cadres who work among the masses. Newspapers are the organs of education, propaganda, and mobilization, which aim to get people to fill their jobs for the Fatherland. Journals (newspapers) are to help the movement progress; especially true in localities where journalists write, for example, they should write in a way that encourages production, induces spirit, etc. The Association itself:

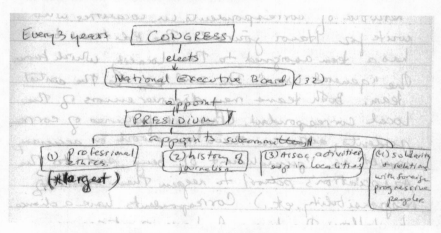

Flowchart illustrating structure of the Journalists' Association.

Actual publication: the Editorial Board of a paper has committees on industrial problems, agriculture, military, defense, education. Each of these subcommittees has special editorial writers who join together to write them.

The main "organization" (control of quality) in the paper is the <u>Control Commission</u> (long argument about what <u>control</u> means, I guess it is validate or verify). The Control Commission must approve all articles for (1) content. The principle is to reflect the truth. Especially during wartime. The news must be proved to be accurate—better to be late and correct than fast and wrong! (For example, verifying American planes downed must be done carefully.) For example, there is a network of correspondents in localities who write for Hanoi journals. The Editorial board has a team assigned to the locality which knows the "general line." The second team is the control team. Both teams may discover errors of the local correspondent. (Frequent failures of correspondents, either in their mass work or accuracy, result in "punishment" of being sent to the Association's school to regain their spirit of responsibility, etc.) Correspondents have a chance to follow the line and have great accuracy, because they are only required to write one article and two news stories per month in the localities. (2) Control Commission also approves grammar. (3) A Readers' Commission receives letters, etc., evaluating reporters, and these are sent to the editorial board.

The following are the major Hanoi papers:
1. Nhan Dan ("The People"). Paper of the Lao Dong. Daily. 120,000.
2. Quan Doi Nhan Dan ("People's Army"). Army paper. Daily. 70,000 (30,000 for Army).
3. Tien Phong ("Vanguard"). Youth Federation paper. Weekly. 50,000. Major force for all youth, male and female.
4. Lao Dong ("Labor"). Trade Union paper. Bi-weekly (2/week). 30,000.

These four, in addition to the Vietnam News Agency and Voice of Vietnam, all have strong control commissions. There is also a weekly meeting of representatives of all the Hanoi papers, to exchange professional and political problems.

Contents of papers
- Editorials: on a yearly basis editorial space is as follows:
  50%: education and mobilization about building socialism (production and economy, science)
  30%: mobilize population to fight with determination and defeat the enemy
  15%: problems of ideology and morality
  5%: international affairs: national liberation movements, socialist forces
- Commentaries have different percentages. For example, more commentary on international tasks

- Specific articles, e.g., production
- "Special hero" columns with stories youth must learn—<u>must</u> be accurate
- News on the South: about ⅓ of material from the Association of Patriotic Journalists in the South is reprinted. (No DRV journalist officially in South.)
- Foreign correspondents in Paris, Cairo, London, Algiers, for various papers.

The Association also has responsibilities with and to the student movement. It helps students form cadres. And has short (6 month) and long (2½ year) range programs for journalists.

The Journalists' Association is distinct from the Department of Information which deals with "talking on the spot" with slogans and posters.

Other comments: Mr. Ky talked a lot in stories and in fact said many fascinating things. I have the impression of a tight press (I think the Control Commission, etc., is a lot more than the copy editor, proofreader, editorial board in most American papers). And it's clear that the newspapers are crucial organs of propaganda in advocating and mobilizing the population. "Propaganda" in the Western sense implies "psychological warfare," but the Vietnamese use it in the traditional Leninist sense, meaning education: "bring truth to the masses" and "inspire good qualities to the masses."

I don't know about the literature—haven't seen it yet and don't know what form of socialist realism it is <u>or</u> what organizations are responsible for authors. Although, I think almost all the current literature is anti-war material. I think it is fairly rigorously controlled (much debate on this point within the American group) and the "control commission" notion seems to exist for literature.

Mr. Ky was so frank about free speech and truth that he was rather disarming. He said at one point that since we know what to ask and what not to ask, we are free to ask what we want!

<u>Comments</u>: (again, he was very free in stating his own views):
- On Catholics: I've nothing against Christ. They've talked of peace for 2,000 years. We've learned it is necessary to fight.
- On Salisbury: better that he visits with a pen in hand than napalm.
- On captured pilots. Most revealing. They are murderers and by Vietnamese traditions, a "murder can only be avenged with the life of the murderer." Yet the pilots are protected with health care and better food than many of our people receive. They were walked

through the streets of Hanoi so the people could see the face of a person who bombs children. Yet they were protected. Is this justice? The U.S. can send bombs to a small country like Vietnam, yet we cannot touch the body of an American person. This was the first time any Vietnamese revealed with such depth of feeling the inner hostility and torture (his own word) about the captured pilots and the absolute injustice they feel at carefully protecting those who have murdered their children. (Quite a sentiment to convey to the American people—could be surprising that all the pilots haven't been killed.)

Final comments—on "armed propaganda" units, they vary, in specialties of speechmaking, leaflets, folksongs, etc. They are self-defense units, carrying guns (rather than guerilla units which fight), and they move to the rear of enemy-occupied zones where their task is to "kill the enemy's distortion of the truth."

- Enough guns in Hanoi to overthrow the social system in five minutes. So what is freedom?
- 3,000 transistor radios were dropped by the U.S. in Quang Binh Province. But they were burned by the population.

Voice of Vietnam:

The propaganda organization was filled in a little more by our discussion, Thursday, 12th October, with the Voice of Vietnam. There we spoke primarily with Tran Lam, Editor-in-Chief, and Mrs. Thu Hùòng, the famed "Hanoi Hannah."[47]

The Voice of Vietnam was founded August 1945, and for the first time used Vietnamese language instead of French names. The signal tune adopted was "drive out fascism."

Objectives: main theme is to defeat U.S. aggression, by leading public opinion and stimulating people to be responsible in their revolutionary duty and to follow the teachings of Ho Chi Minh about the importance of independence and freedom.

People are prepared for a long resistance and cannot expect a fast and

---

[47] Although there was more than one person who broadcast as "Hanoi Hannah," Trinh Thi Ngo (who called herself Thu Huong, or Autumn Fragrance) was the most well known. She broadcast news and music in English from Radio Hanoi to the U.S. troops with the aim of attacking their morale. Philip Shenon, "Hanoi Hannah Looks Back, with Few Regrets," *New York Times*, November 26, 1994, 4

easy victory. The resistance is against a large aggressive power, but there will be ultimate victory.

The motto of the Voice of Vietnam is speak the truth and the news is "controlled" similarly to the newspapers. There must be close watch and military confirmation of "my bai" news. The Voice of Vietnam and Nhan Dan are trusted by the people.

Not clear yet about organizational place of Voice of Vietnam, under what ministry, etc.?

On propaganda for GI's—Hanoi Hannah is the speaker on these broadcasts, daily, to the GI's (1 program transmitted twice a day). Their goal is to state the truth. They recognize the distinction between American friends and the U.S. aggressors. The latter has great wealth and power, and uses its might against a small, poor, agricultural nation. Yet individual GI's are seen as victims of the U.S. policy. Youth is used as "cannon fodder" by the administration. They are taught that Vietnam means Viet Cong, that Vietnam threatens U.S. security.

In another month, they hope to have ready a transmission for the U.S. We talked a while about the difficult problems of establishing effective propaganda for the GI's. What will they listen to? The same problem appeared when we tried to think of a tape we could make which GI's might listen to. Their language was surprisingly good. The music was a strange mish-mosh, ranging from 1950 popular music to Pete Seeger to old-time jazz. (We heard a few of their tapes.) Rennie and Norm talked with them some about specific content and problems of their propaganda.

I'm going to tape an interview with Hanoi Hannah, for possible use in the States. Emphasis on personal background, and her sensitivity to the problems of what alternatives to offer GI's.

Wednesday evening: meeting with the Intellectuals against the Horrendous War Crimes and Hostilities of the U.S. Aggressors (or some such title). A very different experience: roomful of perhaps 40 people, ranging in age from 20 to 70, and in jobs from artist, actor, sculptor, to lawyer, doctor, technician, to university professor and journalists. I thought the group was old, was struck by the lack of women (except a few artists), and noticed a French influence: clothing, hairstyles, shoes, and, in particular, a kind of physical laziness I hadn't seen before (some stodginess, but distinct lack of the remarkable physical trimness characterizing so many Vietnamese).

Not sure of the purpose of the meeting. Oanh had intimated we were there to mildly "goose" them but am not sure. Nor am I sure of their role in the society, except for knowledge that there was some repression in the late 1950's.

We gave 2 speeches:

Bob Allen on the general state of the anti-war movement with some focus on the black movement; and Jock Brown with a fairly sentimental piece about the dilemmas facing middle-class intellectuals. They reminded Jock, who has been reminded of this a half dozen times, that it is the job of Americans to change America. (He frequently invites Vietnamese to come to the U.S. and help our struggle, a serious distortion of the general line!)

They asked some questions (attitudes of American workers? future leadership of U.S. anti-war movement? coordination between black and anti-war movements? U.S. understanding of the war?).

The evening was not terribly interesting, but it made me wonder about one thing a good deal: seems to me that many of our questions must often sound stupid, unintelligent, and naïve. Who knows how many of the things we've asked are questions that could easily have been answered by some reading. I talked with Hieu about this some; he acknowledged that there are things we could read about the government and, particularly, about agriculture which is so unfamiliar to most of us.

Hanoi, Day 14: Thursday, October 12. Premier
Pham Van Dong; evening, captured pilots

Thursday, 12 October 1967

Got up early and went shopping. Walking in the city in the early morning is a good experience. Everything really does wake up at daylight.

Voice of Vietnam at 7:30. Already described.

11:15 we went to see Premier Pham Van Dong. A man of some 60 years, remarkable warmth (like the Mayor), very strong personality. A more elegant setting than usual, but basically the same format as many meetings we've had. He welcomed us and proceeded to make a statement. Most of the substance is paraphrased here as I remember it. (Just changed my mind—decided to type in the combined work we did on a near literal transcript of the talk.)

We only had about 45 minutes. It was worth meeting the Premier, certainly, but I really felt I had nothing very significant to say to him. I felt a kind of humility and a sense of our own insignificance which I hadn't felt so strongly before.

[Beginning of inserted typed statement.]
For October 21ˢᵗ: Premier Pham Van Dong Statement

The Vietnamese people convey their heartfelt sentiments of cordiality to the American people.

These are sentiments of solidarity among comrades in arms, because both the American and Vietnamese people are struggling for a common aim: to oppose the U.S. administration's war of aggression against Vietnam.

For the Vietnamese people, this unjust war encroaches upon our sacred national rights. For the American people, it causes great harm in all fields, political, economic, social, internal, and external, and runs completely counter to the American people's interests.

For our part, the entire Vietnamese people are determined to carry on this long and hard patriotic war, and are firmly convinced that final victory will be ours.

We, Vietnamese people, thank our friends in the United States who are supporting our just struggle. We wish great successes for the movement in the USA to oppose the war of aggression in Vietnam, a movement which is developing both in depth and breadth with each passing day.

We are confident in you, friends! You are fighters of a great people who, two centuries ago, promulgated the "Declaration of Independence," a people who love freedom for themselves and for all other peoples the world over.

You and we are struggling for a noble cause, that is, friendship between our two peoples on the basis of equality, mutual respect, and mutual understanding.

The following is the more complete, paraphrased statement, as I recall it from notes (no official approval):

The Vietnamese people express their sentiments of friendship to the American people. These are sentiments of solidarity among comrades-in-arms, because the Vietnamese people and the American people have a common aim: to oppose the U.S. war of aggression against Vietnam. For the Vietnamese people, this is an unjust war which violates our sacred national rights. For the American people, it causes great harm in all fields, political, economic, and social, and runs counter to the American people's interests.

We must maintain our solidarity. We should coordinate our struggle. We have our work and our task. You have your work and your task. If we each do our work, we will have solidarity and coordination.

We hail your struggle. We have confidence in you and your way of struggle. Two centuries ago your people promulgated the "Declaration of

Independence," a great contribution of people who love freedom for themselves and for all other people the world over. And now the anti-war movement is surging. This marks a new development that it is in the interests of the American people, their internal interests, their external interests, to end the war.

We, the Vietnamese people, will be victorious. It will be our victory, and it will be your victory. There is no reason for not having friendly relations between our peoples. And we welcome this spirit in you.

We are forced to fight, to struggle in this unjust war. We will fight and struggle until we have victory. Victory is achieving our national rights. We are prepared for any form of aggression by the U.S. and we are ready to sacrifice in our struggle.

Time is on our side. We are fighting, we are relying on our own strength, but we attach great importance to the support of peoples of the world, especially the American people. Our struggle is related to the interests of other peoples, including Americans.

The more we fight, the more support we get. And the more isolated the U.S. aggressors become. So our perspective is confidence. And you have our respect in your struggle. You and we are struggling for the noble cause of friendship between our two peoples, on the basis of equality, mutual respect and understanding.

[End of inserted typed statement.]

After the official "statement," he reiterated his belief in friendship with the American people. And asked each of us to speak a few words on the appropriate matter: Carol and Vivian on women, Norm as a journalist, etc. He responded to me that we must increase the solidarity between the American and Vietnamese women. He continuously stressed that our work is in the U.S—that is where our responsibility lies. "Your society must change. I don't and won't live in 'The Naked Society' (Vance Packard)."[48]

He reiterated that they distinguish between the American people and the U.S. aggressive authorities who are waging war. He wished success to all taking part in the anti-war struggle and the struggle against bad conditions in the U.S. "We have confidence in you."

Finally, on behalf of President Ho Chi Minh, he presented us each with

---

[48] Vance O. Packard, *The Naked Society* (New York: David McKay & Co., 1964). Packard examined the invasion of privacy of U.S. citizens by corporations and government.

a rose, symbolizing freedom and friendship. And a promise for militant solidarity.

Dynamic man. Strong leader. Powerful personality. Alert, sensitive, inquisitive eyes and face. So hard to say much more.

After lunch the Voice of Vietnam guys came over with some sample tapes. We listened to Hanoi Hannah, and music. Already commented on that.

Thursday evening we saw captured pilots. All this was in several ways one of the shakiest, unnerving experiences. Walked into the room with Major Bai, some other Army people, a crew of guys with blinding camera lights, and a semi-circular chair arrangement. We saw three men.

1. Elmo Clinnard Baker, Major. Born 25 January 1932 (35 years), Moreland, Missouri, lives in San Antonio with wife and 2 kids. He arrived at Takhli, Thailand, 6 June 1967. Was flying an F105D bomber when shot down 22 August 1967 over Ha Bac Province. Broke his leg in 3 places on landing, and now has a cast from his rib cage to the ankle of his left foot. Was hospitalized post-operatively one month, and has been out just 2 weeks. Must stand with the aid of a crutch—can't sit. Will have cast on 2 more months, and at least 1 (of 3) pins in his hip for one year.

We were warned that he is still frightened; his psychology is upset because of his recent capture, and that we shouldn't ask too many questions. "Don't shake his mental" was the translation we got!

In fact, he did look scared. Jock jumped on him eagerly (that was very bad). He looked nervous, didn't say much. Asked if there are new peace negotiations in the air, what about statements and positions of other countries, the World Series. A little about his health; said he was receiving excellent medical care, food was okay, and he'd been given several things to read, on request. (Felix Greene's Vietnam, Vietnam,[49] some Vietnam Couriers, the same material given to the other pilot who we learned was Baker's roommate.) Didn't ask him about his being shot down and his capture.

Didn't have very strong impressions of him one way or the other. Felt sorry for him with such a miserable injury, but felt the fear wasn't able to be overcome in that situation.

Cameras didn't help. Although we did agree that pictures weren't to be taken during actual conversations (and they weren't), the entrance and exit pictures even made me squirm. (We were the first Americans he has seen.)

---

[49] Refers to Felix Greene, Vietnam: In Photographs and Text (Palo Alto: Fulton Publishing Co., 1966).

2. Douglas Brent Hegdahl (the famous sailor who fell off the ship). Serial number B626330. Born 3 September 1946 (21 years). Watertown, South Dakota. Enlisted in the Navy on 25 October 1966 at Fargo, North Dakota. Left San Francisco 3 February 1967, arrived in Tokyo, went to Clark A.F.B. Philippines. Went to Subic Bay 7 February 1967 and boarded the USS Canberra. Captured 5 May 1967.

A very young kid, dressed in striped maroon and purplish pajamas (like Baker), looking thoroughly "discombobulated" throughout the discussion. He described the amazing tale of having fallen off the ship (in spite of a guard rail) in pitch black darkness, being in the water 5 hours, and finally being found by a fisherman who took him to military authorities.

A strange kid, in some way the nerviest. He couldn't keep his mind on anything for more than 5 seconds. But he did ask, at different times, who sent us, who financed us, and whether we were Communists. He also asked about the movement, about baseball, negotiations (country-by-country), the presidential election. He also said he doesn't like Stokely Carmichael,[50] and that undoubtedly we were receiving much better food.

He seemed a paradox—maybe a logical paradox? Major Bai reminded him that he'd had many questions and urged him to ask them. It's understandable he would forget them, but it nevertheless seemed strange. He had a tape for his family which we are to mail, but he didn't want me to contact his brother in Cleveland. He has seen other Americans—Dellinger[51] and the 3 W.S.P.[52] people.

---

[50] Stokely Carmichael led the Student Nonviolent Coordinating Committee (SNCC), a militant youth organization whose aim was to end segregation, during the mid-1960s.

[51] David Dellinger was an active leader and participant in several antiwar organizations during the Vietnam period. Following the 1968 Democratic National Convention in Chicago, Dellinger was indicted and tried as one of the "Chicago 8," along with McEldowney's travel companions Tom Hayden and Rennie Davis. For more on the events at the Democratic National Convention and the trial of the "Chicago 8," see DeBenedetti, *An American Ordeal*.

[52] Women Strike for Peace, an organization of mostly middle-class, white women, which organized demonstrations against the proliferation of nuclear weapons and the American involvement in the war in Vietnam. Three members of the organization visited North Vietnam in 1967 and met with American prisoners of war held in Hanoi. Amy Swerdlow, *Women Strike for Peace: Traditional Motherhood and Radical Politics in the 1960s* (Chicago: University of Chicago Press, 1993), 218–19.

He's also been out in the city more, museums a little. I didn't care for him particularly, was bothered by his seeming vacantness, and couldn't tell if he was playing a role or not, nor did I puzzle out the significance (if any) of Major Bai encouraging him to speak.

I did very little talking during this interview, also. (He kept rubbing his eyes in a strange, nervous manner.) Spoke of reading the same material on Vietnam that the others did.

3. The last guy was the most horrendous experience for me. Larry Edward Carrigan, Captain. Serial number FV3119604. Born 13 August 1940 (27 years), Arizona. Enlisted 1 June 1962. Pilot of F4D (non-bomber?), took off from Udorn, Thailand (arrived there 28 May 1967). Shot down over Yen Bai Province 22 August 1967. Father of 3.

An astonishing guy. Young, attractive, very healthy, smooth, self-composed and self-possessed.

He aroused in me every conceivable mixed, ambiguous feeling. He had us on the defensive, especially Rennie, asking us to defend our anti-war attitudes, etc. He described his position and capture: usually a test pilot, out of Thailand (has been acknowledged base for 1 year), on first bomber mission. The last of 4 planes, was hit by a SAM [surface-to-air missile]. Said pilots fear SAMs—when they work, they really work. Was in the jungle 3½ days before he was captured. He said the pilots "cross their hearts" when flying "package 6"—Hanoi—(there are 7 "packages"). Usually, he said, U.S. planes don't fly low enough for rifles—fear in the North is missiles and AAA [anti-aircraft artillery]. Strafing and napalm in the South—not the North. CBU's used for flack (dispersing smoke caused by anti-aircraft). Used a lot of military jargon ("max time," "roged," etc.). Mentioned that perhaps would be 350–400 pilots returning to the U.S. when the war ends. Talked a lot about the Geneva Agreements—first thing which made me wonder.

After a while, I didn't believe anything he said (and I withdrew). He "knew" we were Communists; and I knew in the U.S. he would be an enemy, a typical air force trained anti-Communist sharpie. I really hated him—saw him as the white guy from the Southwest who would drop bombs on Negroes in a race riot. The other Americans also seemed eager to get into a "conversation" with him, which I simply could not see doing. (Did say his treatment was good.)

A lot of feelings welled up. First, his being American did not make me feel any kinship (because of the kind of American I suspect him to be). Second, the presence of Oanh in particular, and my consciousness of him, made me think "some of the Vietnamese are my friends; this American is a killer." But the feeling was even more complex, because I did <u>not</u> feel that closeness with Major Bai and the Army people. Jock, at the end, analyzed the pilot's personalities to Bai, which I found absolutely distasteful and unnecessary—and I felt for the first time that we were being <u>used</u> by them for their own propaganda. I knew that, naturally, before even meeting the pilots, but I was aware of a narrow line we had to draw—hate the pilots as I may, it is still a betrayal at the worst and unnecessary at the least (of the kinds of people we are) to be operating politically at the level of helping the Army deal with the American prisoners. I think we have no role in that, beyond a willingness (maybe) to see them. It is madness to assume we can "re-educate" them or tell the Vietnamese how to.

Also learned that the Peace Committee and the Military have enormous trouble arranging this. The problems of transporting the pilots is serious. And they hate them, don't want to watch them. Oanh, we learned, finds it tortuous. His sister's husband (married recently) was killed a month ago by a bombing (5 days after marriage). And it's a torture for all of them, but they've accommodated to the American requests to see prisoners. (Oanh: "I can't stand it.")

Useful information we learned—not much new. Health is obviously good and conditions <u>must</u> be reasonable. They are allowed to write one letter a month. Most interesting: they are totally segregated and know nothing about other prisoners.

[Beginning of inserted typed account by Jock Brown.]
* * * * * * * *

Thursday, October 12, 1967: Interview with U.S. prisoners (Jock Brown notes)
1. Elmo Clinnard Baker. Brief interview, 20 minutes, mostly discussion about his health, broken hip. Some desultory questions about U.S., possible ending of the war, who we represent. Didn't seem interested in anything we had to say. (Rest of Jock's notes on him already written down, or are descriptive of him personally, rather than accounts of our limited conversation.)
2. Douglas Brent Hegdahl. (The sailor who fell overboard from the U.S.S. Canberra, and seen once by Dave Dellinger.) The following are Jock's notes representing answers to numerous questions and his voluntary statements.
    "A gong gets us up at 5. We have showers almost every day; we have

toothpaste, blankets, mosquito netting. We get some exercise most days, work making charcoal, etc. Have seen movies several times. I have been taken to the war museums, where they showed me a bomb crater. I saw some victims of bombing in hospitals—an 8 yr. old boy and a 64 yr. old man—but didn't actually see the man. I have read Felix Greene's Vietnam, Vietnam and Warbey's Vietnam, the Truth.[53] I see the Vietnam Courier. I think there haven't been as many air raids on the city as earlier, how about you people? I sent two letters to my folks and got two back. They feed us pigback (pigfat?), pumpkin, rice, bread. One day we had turkey, I think. My weight is normal, maybe a little over. We make out okay. No, I can't say how many others are with me. I met the 3 U.S. women who were here. What about the '68 elections? What is the U.N. doing? Have any of you people been to South Dakota? I went out on the town once, saw the parks. (About his capture): I was out washing the gun chute, it was pitch black; I don't remember falling. Suddenly I was in the water, couldn't shout, and the ship kept going by pretty fast. I was in the water about 5 hours—I like to swim, it was pretty cool, I used my jacket as a preserver. I was picked up by a fisherman, and when we got to shore and the militia men, I had to walk a pretty long way to the jeep.

What organizations are all you people from? Are any of you Communists?"

Says he might go to college when he returns. He joined the Navy so he would "not have to march." Lots of his friends have been drafted. Major Bai's comment at end: "It is hard to say if he is in better spirits than before. I understand him better than you do. From the Philippines on, he acts simply like a machine. We have been trying to give back to him the vitality of youth. He argued with me once. There is nothing paradoxical about his psychological state, it has a logic in itself." (Trouble with translation here?)

3. Larry Edward Carrigan. By far the most interesting interview. (See separate notes for personal details.) Almost immediately began to quiz us. Found out Carol M. is from Cleveland. Said he was told by the 3 American women he saw that a Cleveland paper had an anti-war poll, but "what I want to know is what circulation does it have." To Rennie: Why are you against the war? No, I'm not asking about your organization, why are you yourself? Are you others against war generally or just this one? I read Felix Greene's book here, it kind of changed my mind. No, please

---

[53] Refers to William Warbey, *Vietnam, the Truth* (London: Merlin Press, 1965).

don't use my name, they've got prisons in the States also, you know, boys. I was really quite ignorant before I came here. I was just flying a plane— kind of a glorified truck driver. I used to argue with guys in the squadron about the war. But you understand, so long as you're in service you take orders from the guy that outranks you. I went to school at Arizona State in Tempe. We're liberal there, this Communist came and they let him speak. (Question about his knowledge of demonstrations, and opinion). Sure, we knew; at Flight School there were 2 guys from Berkeley who told us about the demonstrations. We figured it was something to do on Saturday afternoon, get together and paint a sign. I remember Econ class, the guy used to sit next to me, all of a sudden next week he wasn't there, got drafted. You look at this guy's notes, then he isn't there, it starts you thinking. Demonstrations are great. But do you really think they do any good? (Tries a little to persuade us they don't.) What about the elections? Who will be the Republican candidate? (Expresses surprise when we say "no dove.") What about Romney? Reverend, what about Reagan? What are you doing back home to educate people about the Geneva Accords? (He went on and on about this. . . .) I know our representative at the Geneva Accords in 1954 didn't sign . . . but what do people know about the agreement, article 12, etc.?[54] Felix Greene has it all in his book, and it's all put together in the back so you can find it. (Question from Vivian: will they say you've been brainwashed?) I don't know what the military will say, but do I seem brainwashed (laugh); I was never brainwashed. (On reading materials.) My roommate Elmo (you've met him) is sick; they put me with him to help him get around. After you've gone through each other's wife, kids, baseball scores . . . you run out of things to say. So we asked for something to read. They never gave them to us. We asked for them. They gave us 5 books, 3 magazines, copies of Vietnam Courier. They're all slanted; but before I had the other side. They never asked me to say anything about the government, they never quizzed me about what I read or told me to read it again. When 350–400 people are going through the same thing it's bound to have some effect. I've never seen another [prisoner] but me and my roommate. But I suppose others ask for

---

[54] According to *The Pentagon Papers*, article 12 of the Geneva Accords required all nations participating in the convention to "respect the sovereignty, the independence, the unity and the territorial integrity of [Cambodia, Laos, and Vietnam], and to refrain from any interference in their internal affairs." *Pentagon Papers*, 1:573.

things to read, and they are given things as I was. When I go home as a civilian, the reporter will ask me, Larry, what really happened, and I'll tell him. I'd be in trouble if only I said it (i.e., referring to being "convinced" by Geneva Accords), but it'll be different if there are a lot of guys saying the same things.

(Major Bai told Bob Allen he could ask Carrigan some of the questions he had wanted to tape answers to, and Bob tried, but wasn't able to get through them.) (Bob asked about Carrigan's being shot down.) "Biggest thing that ever happened to me except my wedding night." I was a test pilot to keep the MIG's off the photo plane (reconnaissance?). I was shot down 55 nautical miles from Hanoi. Target was a railroad yard, 4 or 5 parallel tracts NW of Hanoi, which is pretty big for here. There were 4 planes in the mission and I was number 4. They always put the least experienced man in no. 4. I've been a test pilot; this was my first bombing mission (remember, in the air force 7 years!). We had maps and aerial photos of the targets. (Question on weapons.) The CBU is a flak-suppression weapon. I've seen films on it. (No response to Vivian's remark that they kill people or someone else's that they can't go through wood.) I was coming down 600 knots true, max fast. You don't have time to dodge stuff coming past you, so we try to suppress the flak. No, we don't strafe or use napalm in the North; planes don't come in that low. Purpose of bombing is to stop the flow of traffic north and south. (Has it worked?) Well, all night we've been hearing that train whistle outside. Do you think it has worked? (Question: were you briefed beforehand on how to behave if captured?) Now that question really puts me on the spot (no answer).

Continues description: there we were coming down max fast on military thrust from 18,000 feet in pod formation 7 nautical miles from the target. I looked up following my lead and saw this cylinder SAM hit the lead, and it (same one?) hit me. The plane started rolling. The kid in back (no. 2) said, begging your pardon, oh shit. There was smoke in the cockpit, rolling plenty trouble. I decided I had had it and punched off the canopy. A guy just out of flight school would hit the first thing. I'm a test pilot, spend my time flying crippled craft to find what's wrong with them. I jumped out 22 G's. Hit the ejection seat. Things worked as advertised. Don't know if the kid in the back got out. I pulled the beeper out, talked to my lead. I said "see you after the war." He said Roger. I landed in the jungle, talked to some other craft going over and again next morning. Was in the jungle 3 ½ days, one vine after another. Max tired. When I came in there were about 30 people around me, everyone had a gun. I tried to escape and evade but you can't with 30 people. Could have tried to shoot my way out . . .

(On Thailand): oh, yes, they admitted that a year ago, but at first they called us advisers. Our missions don't worry about rifles unless we get forced low. Understand, this just applies to "package 6" in North Vietnam (i.e., Hanoi). Yes, we fear the SAM's. Of course there are lots of bugs in them: sometimes they just go up and come down again. They can either fire them like a bullet or give them a good lock on the target—you go this way and they follow you. Bad country for ground fire. You haven't got enough eyes to follow the lead and spot the bursts from everywhere. SAM's, Triple A, MIG's. No, I don't think we're running out of pilots. A guy gets shot down . . . they send another in. (Question about schedule). We're up before the sun, by a gong. We clean the room, make the bed. They have a honey bucket in the room overnight for discipline (??). We empty it about 7. They give us a cigarette. We have a bath about 5 days a week, shave every 2 or 3 days. We get a real good meal about 10:30, another about 4:30. Work outside most days. Pull grass, make charcoal. Gets your mind off. Do I think about my wife? Are you kidding? Bed at 8:30. (What kind of treatment did you expect?) Different, to be hanging up on a pole somewhere. What it comes to we're sitting out the war. Being well treated. Remember everything I say is a minority of 2. I can only speak for me and my roommate (you've met him, Elmo Baker). I never once had to say anything against the government.

He is encouraged to take the whole pack of cigarettes and candies for himself and his roommate; smiles slyly, saying "I know what you're trying to do to me!"

Conclusion was a lengthy misunderstanding (we think) between Tom's statement of his opinions about the interview, and Major Bai's reactions. See notes on this; haven't copied Jock's notes because mine covers most of the content. One thing Major Bai did say: "I know something of diplomacy and could talk with you in diplomatic terms. But I talk frankly. You came with a great intention which I respect. But if you can't understand the facts, how can the American people? It is not my job to blame you. Because of these problems, we met in Czechoslovakia. We are aware of the difficulties in your country. It is the nature of a soldier to speak frankly." (Again, all this referred to their assumption that Tom was questioning whether the pilots were being honest about their treatment by the Vietnamese. See notes.)

[End of inserted typed account by Jock Brown]

The catastrophe came when Tom spoke at the end, in response to Major Bai's request for "our opinions." He wanted to say: we believe the pilots are receiving good treatment; no doubt about that. But we don't believe other things they say (how much is from their "survival kit when captured") and don't know how to evaluate that. But it was said poorly, and he also used the example of the Stratton photo[55] as bad propaganda, and spoke of the gap between the way the pilots actually speak and what they write in published interviews. And the translation was bad.

Major Bai launched into a long indictment, telling us that Dellinger, the 3 WSP women, etc. all had "proper opinions" after seeing the pilots. He told us their "error" with the Stratton photo was a small error. The situation really was beyond repair. In talking with Oanh later, even he had misunderstood Tom's intentions. It was later cleared up (and we were given 30 letters from prisoners to mail) but it provoked a long discussion among ourselves about the usefulness of seeing captured pilots—much disagreement about how useful it is in the States. My own view, now, is that it's not essential to verify their decent treatment (that's been done), and the issue of prisoners is not a good organizing issue. That is, we are so unsure of our feelings towards them (are they killers? do they use "survival" training when captured? are they liars? are they decent? what should their treatment be?) that not much can be said to the American public about them, except that (1) the Vietnamese do not consider them POWs but captured war criminals, (2) their treatment is at least as humane as that of any other prisoners in history, and (3) it's remarkable that any Americans at all have been able to see them. Very important not to let ourselves be put on the defensive on this issue. After all, it takes incredible nerve to ask them, in the middle of war, to go through all the necessary military and security precautions to let peace-movement Americans see them, even if it's useful to their propaganda (and I'm not convinced they give a damn about that).

The others don't all agree with me, by any means. Rennie thought the guy was sincere (Carrigan), Jock thought it was important to see prisoners. We did agree that it was not worth it if it really created great problems for the Peace Committee.

---

[55] Lieutenant Commander Richard A. Stratton was captured by the North Vietnamese when his plane crashed on January 5, 1967. A photograph of him bowing to his captors and confessing to war crimes against the Vietnamese people was publicized broadly by North Vietnam. Scott Blakey, *Prisoner at War: the Survival of Commander Richard A. Stratton* (New York: Penguin Books, 1979).

Hanoi, Day 15: Friday, October 13. Departure day postponed;
Xunhasaba (Export-Import House); noon, banquet

Friday, 13 October 1967

(Day of departure to be, but not, as it happened.)
Got up early, went shopping. Again, seeing the city move early in the morning is a good experience.

a.m. Xunhasaba (Export-Import House). Ngo-Duc Mau, Director; Nguyen Si Truc, Deputy Director. This is the state firm which exports books, cultural materials in foreign languages; and imports. Purpose: to discuss distribution of material in the U.S. Currently, their material goes officially only to China Books and Periodicals (a distributor?) in California (regularly, they are licensed orders on request); and to some organizations (Liberation, National Guardian); and individuals upon request. Their proposal is to establish the National Guardian as an official agency for distribution. (If possible, other groups in different states or regions could also be licensed.) We know nothing about this; there are dozens of practical questions but maybe the Guardian will do something.

They also would like to find an American publisher to translate a Vietnamese history from French.

(They also loaded us down with beautiful gifts.) And fancy food.

Friday noon: banquet (buffet style) with many of the people we've met, incredible mounds of delicately arranged food, a lot of speeches but, surprisingly, less toasting than expected. Professor Tuong presided—big person, it turns out, in the Peace Committee. People keep turning up in unexpected places and positions—can't place them.

Miscellaneous events: wrote a brief article for Thong Nhat (Mr. Vy's paper). Made me realize how hard it will be to write "credible propaganda" in usable English. (Beautiful ivory, carved necklace as a gift.) Also taped an interview with Thu Huong ("Hanoi Hannah"). It was disappointing. She apparently does not write her own material, and was surprisingly inflexible. Answers were a mixture of poor and cagey. (Saturday Bob Allen and I went over the transcript, and decided we would request permission for minor revisions and additions.)

The ICC plane did not arrive. Departure now scheduled for Tuesday, October 17th. I wasn't particularly upset. Just don't expect much to happen the next four days.

Took a long walk in the evening. Bob Allen and I walked up along the dike near the bridge, sat and watched it for about 30 minutes. Steady stream of traffic across, many, many small trucks and jeeps, mainly empty, some with fuel. Came across the bridge and down the road by the dike. Railroad section still isn't fixed. Surprisingly, all traffic in one direction only. Possibly it's routed that way, to avoid two-direction jam-ups; possibly only one lane is in use now. But the steady stream of traffic was dramatic. We discovered that we were sitting on top of what was once an anti-aircraft installation (probably heavy machine gun), and could see several others. The anti-aircraft has probably been moved closer to the bridge, and to a less exposed area. Couldn't date it. Walking back along the dike also noticed a lot of trucks, construction equipment (sewer pipes?) and rocks piled up along the rise of the dike. But couldn't tell the probable use. We were both again struck by the remarkable fact that we could walk so long through the streets of Hanoi, at night, without being stopped.

(Everyone cracked a little tonight, dreaming up the things we could do until Tuesday and wondering how long we would really stay!)

Hanoi, Day 16: Saturday, October 14. Peace Committee; evening, National Library

Saturday, 14 October 1967

8 a.m. woken by air alert. 9:15 a.m. second air alert (first since Monday).
Morning: meeting with Peace Committee to make schedule suggestions.
3 p.m.: meeting with Peace Committee again, with following proposed plan:
    Saturday afternoon: optional, Museum of Revolution
    Saturday evening: National Library
    Sunday a.m.: Fine Arts Museum
    Sunday evening: Vietnam Courier
    Monday a.m.: Voice of Vietnam
    Monday 2:30: meet with journalists of several newspapers
    Monday evening: visit night school
Also possible: talk to Minh about economy. See Vietnamese documentaries, more contact with Xunhasaba.

3 p.m. air alert

After dinner, Norm, Bob, Vivian, and I walked over to the National Library, ushered by Mr. Phem. Nice building—people really didn't look at us very much. And we didn't wander. Later went for walk with Norm, Vivian, and ventured into an interesting area, walking along the dike. Took a road that crossed the dike towards the river. Narrow, camp-like sites on either side, with entrance gates. And red stars. Maybe camp for road brigades? A lot of lumber there and we could hear some small machinery in operation. Couldn't really tell what it was, and we got a little nervous about venturing too far.

Hanoi, Day 17: Sunday, October 15. Discussions with Jean-Pierre Vigier about weapons; Nguyen Minh of the Trade Union Federation

Sunday, 15 October 1967

Took a long walk in the morning, along the dike, up to the old evacuated market. The pagoda I saw there the other day (at Phô Hang Khoai) in fact is near a bombed area, and its roof caved in as a result of vibrations from the bombing. Walked back into the street quarters more—parallel but west of Phô Hang Dáo, and eventually got a little lost. I communicated with sign language, maps, and a few words of Vietnamese where I wanted directions to, and he promptly piled me on his bicycle and rode me to Hoa Hoãn Riem (lake near the hotel). Upset me a fraction but not seriously. Anyhow, the back streets seem to have more small industry (it's less evacuated than near the market, which is deserted). I think, also, I may've been close to the railroads. Maybe will explore tomorrow.

Afternoon: discussion with M. Vigier about weapons. Will write later. Evening: very useful discussion with Nguyen Minh about income and living costs for workers, rationing, and a little on production and distribution. Will detail later.

(written Monday, 15 October 1967)

For some reason Nguyen Minh (who is a very high-up official in the Trade Union Federation) was willing to spend time answering a lot of "low-level" questions about working conditions, rationing, etc.

I. Income

There are 3 basic forms of income: wages, allowances, supplementary income.

(This is for factory workers)

1. Wages: There are 7 grades of workers. 1st grade is the simplest work, 7th grade is the most difficult. A 1st grade worker (apprentice) gets Đ35/month, 7th grade gets Đ105/month.

    Factory workers are often paid on a piecemeal basis, depending on the type of work. (For example, much mechanical work, textile). On piecemeal basis 1st grade worker can earn up to Đ55/month.

    Wages are set by the Ministry of Labor.

2. Allowances

    a. For city residents, e.g., Hanoi: 12% of wage level; for mountainous regions: 20% of wage level

    b. Special working conditions, such as heat in steel, iron, blacksmith shops: 8–12% of wage level

    c. More than 2 children: 5Đ for each extra child (3 and up)

    d. "Family difficulty": includes damage from bombing, fire, flood; death of child or parent, grave illness. Depends on amount of damage: can get at least Đ10, up to Đ60 per incident, up to 4 times a year. Decisions on amounts made by Trade Union.

    e. Social insurance: includes labor accident, illness, pregnancy. The Trade Union runs a fund—the worker pays nothing. The government fund is 4.7% of its total wage fund. (Don't have amounts.)

    f. Childcare: in general the cost for a child 1 month to 3 years is Đ10/month. The worker pays Đ2/child, and the government pays Đ8. If there are 2 children, the worker pays Đ3 instead of Đ4.

    g. Vacation allowance: 10–15 days per year for workers. They pay 0,^{d}6/day; Trade Union pays travel; guest pays the rest. Teachers, for example, only get 10 days.[56] (This is all pre-war.)

---

[56] In the notations seen here, McEldowney represents the Vietnamese currency (Đ, đ, or dong) in whole numbers and tenths.

3. Other Income

Workers earn extra income by breeding poultry or growing vegetables. Their produce can be sold to the factory collective for the equivalent of 10–20% of their wages. "It is the job of all trade unionists to try to do this." (Also an "unseen allowance" which is scholarships encouraging training for teaching, especially math and physics.)

II. Expenditures

1. Lodging: workers usually live in workers' apartment (1 room). They generally pay 1% of their wages for rent for the family.
2. Utilities: lights, running water, etc. Usually pay 1% of wages/month.
3. Trade Union fees: ½% of wages/month.
4. Clothing: the cost for the rationed amount of cotton per person per month is 0,^{d}75 to 1,^{d}50, depending on quality. Work clothes are provided by the government. For example, work shoes for road brigade, mine, chemical work; on pants and shirts for factory work. The cotton ration is 6 meters/year per person. Extra is allowed for marriage, pregnancy.
5. Food: approximate cost is Đ15–18 per person per month (2 meals per day).
6. Medicine: almost all is provided free, except tonics. The factories pay for medicine when hospitalized and for food (in hospital); worker pays 0,^{d}60/day and the Trade Union pays the other 1,^{d}20.
7. Entertainment: there are fifty Trade Union mobile cinema teams (and entertainment) for workers. Tickets cost 0,^{d}10.
8. Other miscellaneous?

III. Rationing

The chief goods that are rationed are rice, some meat, sugar, and cotton.

1. Rice: minimal for 1 worker 1 month is 13,^{k}5, maximum is 24K, depends on kind of work.[57]
2. Meat: (primarily beef and pork); minimum 0,^{k}7 (700 grams), maximum 2 K.
3. Sugar: minimum ½ K (or 0,^{k}5, 500 gr.) up to 1 K for heavy industry

---

[57] In the notations seen here, McEldowney represents weights in kilograms in whole numbers and tenths.

4. <u>Cotton</u>: 6 meters per person for 1 year. (Extra for pregnancy, etc.; and work clothes provided.)
5. <u>Milk</u>: also rationed to children, sick people, older people.

Rationing is done with a ticket, for example: cotton ration: 6 meters.

		½met			

Each time purchase is made (yardage or ready-made), the card is punched.

These are rations for <u>city</u> workers, I <u>think</u>; am not sure of comparable rations in the countryside where rice is free but some things are not:

Sample	Prices	
Rice	1, ᵏ0	0, ᵈ4
Sugar	1, ᵏ0	2, ᵈ30
Pork/beef	1, ᵏ0	2, ᵈ50 to 3, ᵈ00
Cotton	1 meter	1, ᵈ5 to 3, ᵈ0
Ready-made shirt (state made)		5, ᵈ0

<u>Note</u>: the preceding incomes, expenditures, etc. are for <u>workers</u>. I don't know the corresponding figures for other employment, but sample monthly incomes are:

Minister	200 Đ
Vice Minister	170–180 Đ
High officials	160 Đ of mass organizations (Trade Union, Peace Committee)

(Ho Chi Minh 245 Đ or seven times the lowest factory wage.)

Further explanation on income (from Mr. Pham). Apparently Đ35 is the lowest starting wage across the board. And the highest salary is the President's. There are gradations within each kind of work: in general, there are higher wages for people with university degrees. And within each field, heads of mass organizations are equivalent to Ministers in pay. Still not sure of relative wages by occupation, except that workers are in general at a maximum of Đ105 (janitors to hotel workers to factory workers). But some employees in factories are technicians and therefore on a higher scale.

More examples: usually start at Đ65 with university degree; (Hanoi) technician with high school degree (i.e., technical school) Đ45—but with university degree Đ65 (starting).

Apprentice teacher, Đ55 (3rd degree: 8th or 10th grade), after 18 months, Đ65. Can earn up to at least Đ115. Doctor begins at Đ65, interpreter at Đ65, (but janitor Đ35).

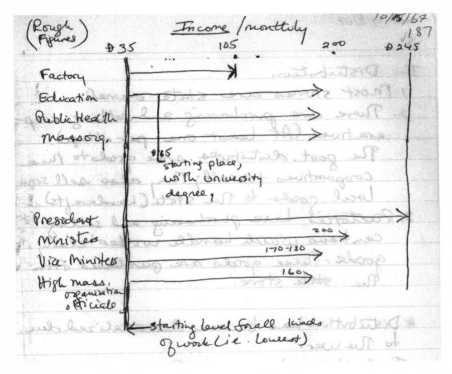

Graph illustrating monthly income.

Production and Distribution

I. Production: state owned; and cooperative. Private production almost non-existent. Agriculture: largely cooperative. Heavy industry: almost 100% state owned. Industry: about 50% co-op; 50% state owned. Government regulates all raw material supply; prices; consumption; production regulations (quality, etc.)

II. Distribution:

1. Most stores are state owned.
2. There are purchasing and selling cooperatives. (At least one per village.) The government distributes some goods to these cooperatives to sell; they also sell some local goods to the state (handicrafts).
3. Factories have purchasing and selling canteens which handle workers' daily goods. These goods are purchased from the state store.

Distribution has become decentralized due to the war. Trade Unions have significant role:

1. Educate workers to practice economy and make goods last! Often consumer meetings are held (attended by state store workers and producers). Consumers discuss (a) equality of goods, (b) distribution methods (example: getting blankets to mountain area before delta region).
2. Encourage members to attend government meetings to set prices, especially of new goods.

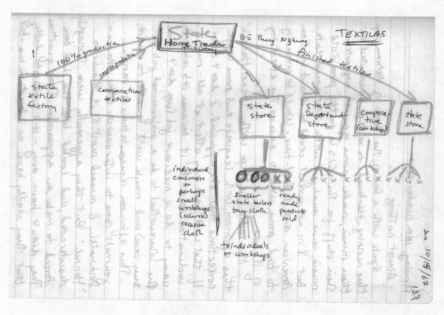

Flowchart of distribution of textile goods.

Monday, 16 October 1967

Almost nothing.

Spoke with a few of the Voice of Vietnam guys this morning; listened to a tape, commented on their music, made some general suggestions. Their stuff for the GIs is pretty poor—old music, news analysis with Vietnamese data. But I'm not sure it could be decent until an American did it full-time. Would be interesting to find some way to assess the effect any of it has.

Also redid the tape with "Hanoi Hannah" this afternoon, with language and some usage corrections that she approved. I don't know if that will have any effect at all—my inclination is to do it because it's relatively easy to do a mediocre job (we don't have the wherewithal to do a professional job in any case) and maybe we'll be able to use it.

This afternoon representatives of various journals came to interview us. Utter fiasco—fortunately I missed most of it thanks to "Hannah." But they apparently were thoroughly disinterested, and looked like they had been forced to make an appearance. Their questions? They didn't have any—it's understandable that they really have no interest in us, but a little surprising, still, that they haven't the vaguest idea of what to do with us. Would be interesting to know who arranged both this session and the earlier one with the intellectuals.

Evening: we had some introduction to the complementary night school system. Our request was to "sit in casually" on a technical school class. We were hosted by a man from the Educational Service (city level of Ministry of Education) who took us to several schools. There are 4 branches: regular school; kindergarten and maternal; teacher training; complementary. The complementary program in factories is organized by the Trade Unions which "create favorable conditions" and may help solve implementation problems.

First visit: night school of a pharmaceutical product factory in Hanoi—over 70% woman employees, much of the factory evacuated. The factory has classes Monday and Thursday nights, 7:00 to 9:45 p.m.; there are 6 classes from 4th to 8th grade. {Classes are either physical science (math, chemistry, physics) popular for technicians, etc.; or social sciences (literature, history, geography) popular for office work, political cadres, etc. The factory classes we saw were primarily the first group.} Approximately 200 are in the classes (18–50 years), which is 98% of the workers. 65% are working towards 3rd degree (i.e., 8th–10th grade). By next year all will have completed 4th grade (or 1st degree).

1st degree—grades 1–4
2nd degree—grades 5–7
3rd degree—grades 8–10

We went barging our way into 4 different classes. Ages varied greatly—in general the youngest were most advanced. Degree of friendliness also varied (greatest among the young people). All the classes, we noticed, received orders to stand and applaud, but in one class laughter and applause at one comment was much more spontaneous. It's hard to tell how much discipline exists in the schools in general; the school at the agricultural cooperative had a good deal of discipline, it seemed. Also noticed that all the teachers in the factory school were men—they are from the factory itself. Indicates something, since the majority of the employees are women yet the teachers are still men. First class we saw: 4th grade, studying arithmetic.

Older people—not much response. 15–20 people?

2nd group—an 8th level math (algebra) class: 47 present, 5 absent—several long benches, and a young male teacher. A giggly class (perhaps the girls were wondering about our clothes?), in which I noticed a "May Bay My" hair comb[58] and laughed, and she presented it to me (made herself, with a peace dove, surprisingly). And another woman asked to send greetings to American women.

3rd: 7th grade, physics, older people (maybe 25–30 people?). Male teacher. Woman from South spoke and for the first time, I had the distinct impression her words were not being translated to us.

4th: a 7th grade class, with maybe 50 people, including several small kids, who seemed to be studying history, or something political.

We later learned that the teachers are paid. 0, d6 per hour for 2nd degree; 0, d8 per hour for 3rd degree. Each student pays 0, d8 to 1, d0 per month.

Evacuated factories in the countryside also are part of the "state plan to improve the workers' education," but conditions there are more difficult due to no electricity, crowdedness, etc. Certain workers, such as railroad workers, have mobile units which they attend 2 days (full) a month and sometimes more.

---

[58] "May Bay" means "airplane" in Vietnamese. "My" can mean "American." The comb is probably made of metal from a U.S. plane that had been shot down.

The second visit was to a night school for that particular district (in a building used as a regular secondary school during the day), that is, 8th–10th grades. We visited an 8th grade chemistry class, about 45 people, very diversified (though mostly young). The teacher is a General Education teacher 20 km. from Hanoi during the day. The "head" of the class put a question to us, formally—it was strained some.

The other classes we passed had men teachers, also, with one exception. A large, 3-story building—many students. (On the way out, we <u>met</u> Tâm's wife who attends there.)

In general it takes 1 year to complete 1 grade—6 hours per week, with 3 subjects a night, September through June. At the 10th grade, a worker can be chosen by the factory to attend the university and get increased technical training. About ½ of factory technicians were trained by complementary schools: from worker to technician! Not sure how a person progresses from the 10th grade to the university if he is in a non–Trade Union night school, who selects him, etc.

It becomes quite possible to believe that the DRV really is wiping out illiteracy and really has the entire population in some form of educational program.

Hanoi, Day 19: Tuesday, October 17. Departure day;
Xuan Oanh discusses guerrilla warfare; drive around
Hanoi; Film Cartoon Studio of Vietnam

Tuesday, 17 October 1967

Departure day again.

Long talk early in the morning with Xuan Oanh (the last). Began by mention of Che Guevara's death,[59] confirmed by Castro, which Oanh thinks is probably (possibly?) a form of adventurism. Either Che didn't have enough support built up in local areas to which guerilla troops were moved, or there were agents. In any case, Oanh thinks that Vietnam-style guerilla fighting is very unlikely in Bolivia (probably in Latin America, in general) and that peasants are not ready to support a guerilla movement.

This initiated a more general discussion of guerilla warfare, a "lesson" one might say? Oanh described guerilla warfare: the need of the guerilla

---

[59] Che Guevara was killed in Bolivia on October 9, 1967.

forces to know the land, to have the support of the people. Vietnamese fighting has become much more sophisticated since the French resistance, in response to all the new methods introduced by the Americans. I tried to pin him down on actual techniques (tunnels, etc.), but he was elusive. But he talked some about "special jobs" reserved for guerillas, example: getting inside an enemy fortification before army plans are laid, to obtain vital information. A crucial point is the joint leadership of the regular military command with the guerilla leadership at certain points: in no other form of fighting does the army command actually make collective decisions. But the role and importance of the guerillas' task—their job of laying groundwork, preparing for a regular army maneuver—is recognized and respected.

Many guerilla fighters enter the army where they learn more sophisticated forms of fighting. (Most?) Army regulars have gone through the steps of guerilla warfare and perhaps local armies, but many expert guerillas remain where they are. That is, guerilla fighting is the most common, low-level form, and most widespread among the population, but some of its techniques are among the most sophisticated.

Battalions are large (Oanh directed one during the French resistance) and maintaining morale is a basic necessity. Therefore, a smaller unit has been developed (on a voluntary basis). This is a unit of 3. Militarily, one man carries a machine gun, one an automatic rifle, and the third a small gun and grenades. But the unit is also "spiritual," for each member is from a different province, and the 3 share not only battle experiences but try to teach each other their culture, and "adopt" their families. Deep loyalties are built. (Oanh still had contact with the other 2 men of his unit from the Resistance.) The unit also fights—or volunteers on missions—together. The "unit principle" is also applied to other levels of fighting: in self-defense squads at agricultural cooperatives, the unit consists of people from 3 different parts of the village (3 hamlets); or the same in 3 sections of a factory. The unit is typical of the Vietnamese effort to have tight relations at the most grass-roots level—an intense form of participation which omits no one and gives each person a stake in what's happening. (Very useful discussion.)

. . . Later in the morning: an air alert with perhaps the most bombing I've yet heard, off in the distance.

Around 10:00 a.m.—a quick drive around Hanoi to see more bomb damage. As we drove I was struck by the contrast between this drive and that of the first day which showed us only peaceful parks and pagodas, and one bombed site. First we passed young girls, along the dike, being trained to use bayonets—preparation for ground invasion. Then sped into the village between the dike and the river, near where we'd walked the day before (the building Norm and I had seen was a welding factory, we learned). The village was crammed (it seemed), and old, and dusty; noticed piled-up bits of aluminum, but don't know what they were. Going towards the bridge, a part of the village had bomb damage. Going away from the river, Phuc Tam street had been bombed; also, Phô Nguyen Thiep, near the market—brick buildings on both sides were badly damaged. Phô Yen Phu bombed in May (don't know section); Phô Le Truc, near Phô Tran Phu, was the site where a U.S. [F-105] Thunderchief was shot down in May. Drove along Nam Bo Street (populous Huan Kiem district) and Phô Ly Thuong Kiet (seemed to have many embassies, also the location of the Peace Committee). Then into Hai Ba section: along Phô Hue, which we'd seen earlier, but now has a sign constructed about the "May Bay My" which hit; and Phô Ngo Thi Hnam (Nham?) which was badly bombed in December 1966. Got a sense of a lot more damage inside Hanoi, we drove so quickly that I have no sense of the geography of where we were (and no map to refer to).

But the over-all impression is incredible: Hanoi is like a mobile factory. All over, every street, are many humming little shops: some have generators, some repair bicycles, but all over the sense of motion. Feverish motion. On many streets there are trucks, some new Russian and Czech, others that are probably pre-war, of the French Resistance (old, old ones). In some areas Hanoi can be described as a huge truck garage—probably many of these trucks don't always run or are in constant need of repair, and they must come through Hanoi. I had the feeling today of many more people in Hanoi—not young children—moving, hurrying, feverishly.

Our last formal meeting was with the Film Cartoon Studio of Vietnam, where we met (a rather young) staff, and had a brief introduction from Truong Quang, director. The Studio, created in 1959 in "response to President Ho's love of children," now produces about six cartoons a year; the first in color is currently in preparation. The contents of the cartoons give children the following advice: (1) love the fatherland and compatriots; (2) learn to study and do manual labor well; (3) have discipline and solidarity; (4) have honesty and braveness; (5) practice good hygiene. In general, all who see the cartoons are educated about revolutionary heroism and the importance of education. Every child in Vietnam sees the cartoons, in cinema houses, mobile units, etc. 1966 was a year of great festivals to show the films. The importance of the studio is expressed by the fact that 1 part of the otherwise-evacuated studio has been ordered to remain in Hanoi.

We saw the studio: an animation desk, sunken in concrete, with Czech-adapted equipment; a marionette workshop (set up for the 1st color cartoon), whose cameras are carefully sheltered when not in use.

And we saw 3 cartoons. The first: "Little Rabbit Goes to School," was a marionette story of speedy rabbit who dawdles and gets to school too late, while the slow tortoise arrives on time (based on legendary tale). The moral: kids, don't wonder too much and wander. Highly moralistic, I thought, but interesting.

Second: "Little Peasant Girl and the Tiger," a folk story done with paper cuts. A little girl outwits a mean tiger and smashes him to death. The moral: powerful enemy can be defeated by wit. The violence is not at all concealed. "Destroy the enemy" is equally the moral (and the tiger, it seemed, was barely provocative!). Done in 1964.

Third: a silver prize winner at Romania, done in 1965, "Little Kitty," testifies to revolutionary heroism. It is written by Nguyen Dinh Thu (Chairman of the Writers Association) and is for adults as well as children. A little kitty, determined to win, can defeat a big rat bully! Fairly sophisticated and well done.

Last—we saw the first few minutes of the first color cartoon, about the "unquenchable spirit" of the people of South Vietnam high plateau, about 2 children who dream of building (as masons) buildings and socialism.

One of the reactions I had to the film studio was the sense of actually seeing progress in the flesh. Christ, the U.S. cranks out so many cartoons a year, of all levels of sophistication (and crap), and here we were seeing the very first effort in color in Vietnam. A step forward. I felt like the films were too moralistic in ways, yet interesting—and I wish I knew how representative they are of other educational forms and how they're greeted. American cartoons condition me to expect (usually poor) humor. Perhaps what I'm after is the visual form of humor in the society.

Pre-departure: brief conversation with Olivier Todd of Nouvelle Observateur, who said some kind words. Our "last supper" was dramatic: we took over the serving completely from Minh Tinh and then took the dishes into the kitchen. I said something to her about our purpose (desire for equality, which of course reflects our bias that most service positions reflect inequality) and she responded by thanking us for our "equal treatment." It dawned on me that "equality" is a word not used often by the Vietnamese, though movement people frequently use it to describe relationships. I was moved by her statement, and by a remark made later by one of the girls at the bar that she would miss us, another rarely expressed sentiment. It's nice to feel that we really acted differently from the usual foreigner in the Hotel Thông Nhat—don't know if that is wishful thinking or not. I do think we tried. I think I was successful in breaking some barriers by my efforts to learn some Vietnamese, on a daily lesson basis, from several of the girls. Who knows, though? On the other hand, they are absolutely experienced in dealing with foreigners, though I indulge myself in thinking that they probably responded a little differently to the first young American women they've met. Departure from the hotel was fast and not very emotional.

We left, via the Long Bien Bridge, as Hieu had promised we would, 2½ weeks ago. The railroad section is still in repair, the auto part is slow and seems shaky at spots. Took a long time. A dramatic last view: going towards Hanoi was an incredible stream of traffic, much of it military, anti-aircraft units, cranes (used to lift SAM's), occasional generators, all camouflaged, all in motion, moving every night to create new patterns on the countryside. Literally this motion occurs daily: anti-aircraft is shot from mobile trucks; SAM's are moved nightly; while U.S. reconnaissance planes desperately try to keep up with the moving scenery.

Airport scene hard. Especially goodbye to Hieu. We strolled outside a little and joked about the part of my heart I'm leaving behind. He'll be a very warm memory (I suspect many of the Americans feel that way, especially because Oanh is harder to talk with easily). More later on this. Farewell flowers. Bits of tears. Hard for them to see another group go, and never really expect to see them (us) again, despite the many promises, hopes. Last fleeting impressions. . . .

Reflections and the Journey Home,
October 18–November 3

Wednesday, 18 October 1967, <u>Vientiane</u>

Crazy crazy reactions to leaving Hanoi. Returning to the "Free World"—Laos, what a place, positively invested with an American presence. Immediately I became suspicious of everyone—saw conspiracies all over. And it happened so quickly—2 hours post-Hanoi, when we arrived at the airport here last night. Varied reactions: genuine confusion about where I am (geographically); keep hearing sounds which I think are air alerts; language problems (mumbling Vietnamese phrases—càm òn, dong chi, tam biệt) to the Laotians at the desk who think I'm crazy. The movement, the transition happened so quickly—just pummeled back into another world in a matter of hours, seeing the U.S. planes all over the Laotian airport, western dress. The appearance on the spot of a <u>Newsweek</u> guy wanting a story—and my assuming every other person must be a CIA agent.

Evening—late—a rather difficult discussion about whether to give a statement to the <u>Newsweek</u> guy. With some bitter feelings, we decided against it, instead to prepare a statement for October 21st.

Went to sleep, wishing very much that I was back in Hanoi, with all the comfort and warmth there (despite the problems). Memory of a ghastly news release (USIA) [U.S. Information Agency] about North Vietnam prisoner propaganda lingers in my mind, firmly identified with Laos.

Wednesday, 18 October 1967, Phnom Penh

The return. Being back makes me want passionately to grip the memory of Hanoi. Such a short distance back, yet so far. . . . Quick, hasty impressions of Phnom Penh by contrast to Hanoi: more heat, more Western influence, and a much slower pace. Much of Hanoi can be dramatically contrasted to Phnom Penh. The streets of Hanoi are narrow, often chopped up, the sidewalks are interrupted by a constant path of shelters, many of them waiting to be installed. Little stores and living units crowd together off the sidewalk, though often one glimpses long, perhaps spacious, alleys back into a central patio. Buildings are aged, though many are newer than they appear. Paradoxically, while the city is relatively empty due to dispersal, it looks crowded; that is partly because many people who used to live on the 2nd floors above their shops now live—all the family—on the ground floor, in the shop, for protection against air attacks. But the architecture, by and large, is rather dingy-looking; the country/city will have a lot of rebuilding to do. Most organizations seem to be housed in large old French buildings, some of which have also been converted into museums. (In contrast, Phnom Penh has a substantial number of new buildings, business and residential.) We saw from a distance the houses of some of our friends—better housing externally (simply homes rather than 2nd floors over stores) but still small. Regretfully we never saw the inside—perhaps not customary for us to be invited in. The parts of the "scenery" that stick fast are the shelters—sometimes lined up 100-long—and the bicycles: 100s of them, all over. Occasionally a car—or a jeep, which use their horns constantly—and flee through the streets dodging bicycles, pedestrians, and occasional pedicabs, but mostly bicycles—largely they are French. Clothing is also striking: very uniform, practically no Western influence (although occasionally Western shoes and jackets appear—some European, some Russian). Many people are in very aged garments, literally patched together. Black and maroon are characteristic colors. Everyone wears sandals, of some form, ranging from Ho Chi Minh sandals made of U.S. plane–captured rubber, to plastic-like sandals, to thongs. Made me realize, especially noticing that everyone dangles bare toes (except the highest dignitaries), how incredibly uncomfortable the Vietnamese must have been in their monkey suits and tight Western shoes at Bratislava. No one in Hanoi wears a suit—exception was a few intellectuals at the meeting we attended. Even the mayor was dressed informally in a short-sleeve shirt, over trousers (though with Western shoes). (And can't forget to mention that beautiful conical hat on nearly every girl, and the abundance of pellet hats.)

Many old people in Hanoi, though I can't begin to estimate age. Vietnamese in general look 5–10 years younger than they are; I don't know if old people age suddenly or of they're even older than they seem. But there were many old people around, selling things (as private sellers?), carrying around baskets on their shoulders, cooking in the streets. Older people were often the least responsive in formal situations—they've just been fighting too long and remember the French too well. Young people in the streets are delightful: lively, but shy, affectionate to each other, friendly and curious both towards foreigners. It is common for girls to hold hands; it is not unusual to see young men holding hands. Girls, in particular, tend to be very giggly, especially when one smiles at them. I found this both in the streets and in some of the more formal places we visited. One sign of change and developing technology is seen in women's hair. Traditionally the women have magnificent long hair, below the waist. Younger women wear it braided, or pulled back, or straight; older women pile it on top of their heads. But sadly, many of the young girls have cut their hair and curled it, and beauty-shops seem to do a thriving business. In some situations the nature of employment demands short hair: in certain factories, in hotels and restaurants. But I suspect many women see it as a symbol either of freedom or of success—a lot of the professional, organizational women we met had short hair. Similarly, some of the more middle-class men (doctors, other intellectuals) wear European hair styles. (More: characteristically everyone carries a small plastic bag, on the arm, on bicycle handles. Probably contains clothing, first aid. But everyone, man and woman, carries them.)

Little children, by and large, are curious about foreigners, and with the slightest smile of encouragement, I found it easy to create pied piper–like followings. Some parents approve; other parents (mostly older people) chased away the kids. But they are still shy and not physically aggressive at all (one of the most remarkable contrasts with Phnom Penh, where they don't hesitate to approach foreigners). Vietnamese kids keep their distance, at least bodily, and often run and hide from "hellos."

Hanoi, of course, is striking for its absence of foreigners. Only a few European journalists—no Americans—and people from socialist countries whom we didn't see because they stay in other hotels, or embassies. But people were either friendly to us, or ignored us—no visible hostility I can recall, even when I got up the nerve to say I was American. In many cases they simply don't seem to care. Walking around Phnom Penh made me wonder what Hanoi would be like in peacetime, what Western influences would be allowed to be present? Cambodia is so damn French—yet DRV shows no signs of the French, except for architecture, people who speak the language, and countless old trucks. A remarkable testimony to the Vietnamese determination to have their culture prevail.

Vietnamese customs left a dramatic imprint on my memory. I, in fact, grew intolerant of them in some situations. Tea ceremonies are a real ritual, and disturbed me at times because the tea pourer inevitably seemed to be a servant-type. No way to get around it. The tea, Vietnamese candies, and fruit (bananas, hông) certainly weren't special for us (everyone eats them); but it got to be unbearable to have pretty girls cramming stuff down our throats, 3 times a day and invariably after large meals at Hotel Thông Nhat. Yet the ceremony served a purpose: frequently the host would give a brief talk, then order a break for tea. We just grew to equate tea with formal meeting and lack of substance—too often the truth. Yet the tea and the fruit are a real Vietnamese tradition and a basic ingredient of the culture. Lots of fruits abound—seen all over—and people make them a basic part of their diet. (Everyone in Vietnam is small—slender—we saw but a few exceptions.) I'll remember the bananas (which I ate by the dozen!), the sweet-smelling trees, and the flowers—another tradition, used for foreigners, but characteristically local as well. Lots of people sell flowers in the market and many people grow them. It's really a friendly and colorful custom!

Other impressions: the noises of the city—they begin early, 5:00 a.m., with a myriad of bell bicycles, some car horns, and occasional loudspeaker announcements. The loudspeakers were dramatically unobnoxious, some music, some news, announcements of approaching "May Bay Mỹ." But they don't blare and their presence is not very constant at all—not to be described as "socialist thought–regulation" coming over as some critics have reacted. In the streets, the bicycles have competition from the numerous small humming machines, all sizes and shapes, and from the sound in places of construction work. Some people hawk their products on the street, but not many or at least not very noticeably. I was struck by how much the noise is that of work, rather than of play and entertainment. (But, also, singing—see next page for belated thoughts.)

In retrospect, one thing I've recalled is the amazing proliferation of written material. Posters, it is true, are fairly uniform, and are propaganda. There are also numerous bookstores, frequent little magazines stands, but most strikingly, there is printed matter all over. Whether it's "plane scoreboards" in street quarters, old men and women with tattered old booklets, young people with advanced technical material, print presides and everyone seems to read. It is an impressive accomplishment of the DRV that illiteracy has almost been wiped out. (I noticed in Phnom Penh that no one at all reads—quite a contrast. Wonder how much of this stems from the difficulty of learning script rather than the Arabic letters.) Another afterthought is the remarkable cleanliness of Hanoi—things certainly look old and dingy in places, but not littered or dirty. Quite a contrast to most cities.

Thursday, 19 October 1967

A whole pressed-together series of strange reactions, thoughts, and comments as the 7 of us finally split up (Rennie, Norm, Bob, Vivian to Paris tonight). No doubt that we've shared a unique experience, not likely to recur. And there are many funny things, little ones, which we'll joke about and use to remind ourselves of Vietnam: farewell greetings, with the characteristic kiss of each cheek; begin a million sentences with " . . . as our beloved President Ho Chi Minh has said . . . ;" remind ourselves that the Vietnamese distinguish between the peace-loving Americans and the American aggressors (probably the most oft-repeated statement!); tell each other Vietnamese proverbs, for we have learned that the Vietnamese have a proverb for every conceivable situation—even if made up on the spot!; give flowers to each other at appropriate moments.

These are remembrances about the country and people themselves. But also—memories about the group of us: will any of us return to Hanoi (maybe to meet in Independence Square to celebrate peace)?; jokes about the hotel services and the trials and tribulations we caused for the always cheerful staff (I really think they liked us—our enthusiasm delighted them at times though our lack of delicacy perhaps left something to be desired!). And for me—when will I ever go 'round the world again???

Friday, 20 October 1967

I am going to complete this in 3 parts—describe the rest of the return trip just to fill out impressions; review some military discussions with Vigier (Sunday, October 15th); and then try to plunge into some of the many thoughts I've had, including those inspired by a number of conversations with my fellow Americans. A long talk with Bob, Norm, Vivian Wednesday evening, October 18th, and a talk mostly with Norm walking around Phnom Penh Thursday, late afternoon, October 19th. This is written partly in retrospect of the past few days.

Now Monday, October [23], 1967, Tokyo

More Hanoi memories came back: singing, it is common, despite the war. Everywhere people sang "Ket Đoan,"—this is the Unity Song (old Chinese melody). It is a frequent phenomenon that the song is sung all over, in the North, almost as an anthem—another indication, perhaps, of optimism about the war ending or Vietnam winning. (Tom said, 2 years ago in the DRV people did not sing "Ket Đoan.") Another thought: the importance of Nguyen Van Troi, the electrician who was executed 14 October 1964, for trying to kill McNamara (I think I've written this already). At any rate, he is an incredible hero in the entire country: aside from the poignant film we saw, there are numerous songs written to his memory and sung by everyone, and celebrations in remembrance of him. (Norman Morrison is also eulogized: he is barely known in the U.S., but suicide for the movement plays a very different role in Vietnam—in the U.S. we would "take someone with us." I think all the Americans found this difficult to understand.)

I have looked back at some photos and am struck by recalling the nature of bomb damage. Especially the starkness of the craters, which are long and deep, and generally filled with water. There was also an isolation around many sites—piled up bricks and debris which suggest the hasty departure of many people. Mounds of very desolate-looking stuff. But while isolated, not barren, not end-of-the-worldish. Enough life still around; in some places the solitude was both broken and dramatized by the little children who ran after us, one with a water buffalo. That made me feel lonely—it made clear that people no longer live or work there.

Back to memory again, suddenly, comes the air alerts. For how long will every whining siren instinctively made me start up? I realize how I'd internalized and automized my reaction to that noise—such a rotten and constant part of the lives of many.

. . . Finally departed Phnom Penh after several dismal efforts. First, typhoon in Hong Kong. Then no plane—left, after all, Friday afternoon, October 20th, at 5:00 p.m. But I walked about the city for a few last times, to firm up my impression. Mostly the impression was one of contrast with Hanoi, as I've said. Westernization all over, dramatized by the face-lifting the whole city is getting in preparation for Jackie Kennedy's visit.[60] Couldn't get into the Prince's Palace, but rather regal from the outside. Flitting memory of the grandeur and austerity of the temple of Angkor Wat, and the

---

[60] Jacqueline Kennedy visited Cambodia in November 1967.

Great Buddha. Noticed, for the first time, a prison—barbed wire and all. And heard the familiar Phnom Penh sounds: cat calls, aggressive kids, some leers. So different. Glad, finally, to leave.

First transit stop: Bangkok. A terror of an experience. A huge, spanking new, American-financed airport, absolutely crammed with expensive goodies to buy. Many U.S. planes (fighter bombers) on the airfield; many Americans inside; an English-language newspaper for the U.S. population ("liberal," pro-war—and keep the U.S. in Thailand to keep back Communism). The free world, as it were. American presence was simply overwhelming, just at the airport.

Wednesday, 25 October 1967

The stretch to Hong Kong was worse, because we were joined by incredibly loud, rude, and bawdy groups (Australians, as it happened) who delighted in harassing the oriental stewardesses. Landed in Hong Kong, a city which really defies description. Lights, lights, lights all over, especially at night. Most of Saturday, 21st October, spent there. Walked around some, enough to get fleeting impressions. The place truly is a colony—no presence—run by and for the West. (Again so incredible that the DRV escaped unscathed by this.) Impressions: it reeks of money, many money odors: perfumes, whiskies, jewelry, plush hotels. Of course the Chinese are desperately miserable. My tourist trip was up Peak Tram, one thousand feet above sea level, to a breath-taking view of the harbor, the financial buildings, the rich folks' mansions, and the class structure, oh so visible from the top of the hill! The best account of the colony comes in a little guide book (British prepared) which warns tourists of the natives' habits, essentially begging, cheating. These little travel brochures turn out to be quite revealing of prevalent attitudes, how they expect to be treated, what they think tourists want. Curiously, I talked to a German (going to the Palace Hotel—airline expense)—immediate prejudice popped up—an industrialist in Indonesia, and he was relatively okay on the war, cautious, said Germany had enough problems, and the U.S. should get out. Restored my faith in trying to "organize" people. Also saw the "little red book" bookstore—filled with Mao posters, etc. Strange, awful place. Don't feel like sketching the politics from such a short view. Was anticlimactic in one way. Walked past what happened to be the American consulate, and saw a small group of (American) students with anti-war signs, and among them was Molly Coye. Joined them for conversation for a bit—feeling sorry for their small size but glad to be among friends and a little lonely about being out of Washington October 21st. Strange irony.

Again, glad to leave—what a bastion of colonialism—more blatant than anywhere.

. . . Arrived Tokyo late Saturday night. Spent three fairly productive days there. Much time with Zengakuren (Student Union), some girls in a dormitory, a little time with the Japan Peace Committee. In general, living the student life rather than the tourist life. Spoke with a number of groups of students one evening in the dormitory, and at a campus. Briefly: arrived Saturday, after great confusion went to Zengakuren office, and Tokyo Fed. Office, and finally to dorm with 2 girls. Sunday (22nd October) talked politics over breakfast, went to Zengakuren office. Spent afternoon walking and talking with Secretary General Ieno, after having Japanese lunch. Had dinner back at the dorm. Terribly shabby living conditions there—apparently a real problem for many university students. That evening talked with 8 girls about Vietnam. Absurd discussion because they all pretended to understand English, and don't. Monday, 23rd October 1967, talked in the morning with the Zengakuren newspaper editor, fortunately with an interpreter. Good discussion. Then the translator and 3 other students from Tokyo University Foreign Studies took me to Wasita University (huge: 40,000) where I wound up talking American movement with the "Circle Club"—a political arm of the school, I gathered. Evening: (post-dinner) talked with Ieno about Japanese student movement; later same evening talked with Jim Polachek—American studying there (name came from Molly Coye in Hong Kong) about the trip. This was the first test of talking without an interpreter for nearly 2 months—a strange sensation and rather obvious, it turned out! Early Tuesday, 24th October, met translator friend Tsuyoshi. We walked around (I really saw a lot of Tokyo from subways and taxis). Then to Peace Committee where I had that familiar game-playing sensation of walking in and appearing to be someone I'm not (a little uninformed American girl, meeting with probable high-bureaucrat officials). But there it was, and the usual discussion took place (helpful, some). Then to Tokyo University Foreign Studies—a really good, warm experience: instantly nearly 30 kids gathered and we had a harried but excellent discussion—largely questions of me but a very spirited session. The head of the student autonomies there, my translator friend (by then an obnoxious hanger-on), and another guy hurried me to the airport, after a collection for taxi fare, in true student breakneck, last minute fashion, like home! Won't try to summarize Tokyo now. One interesting observation, that is about the questions the various student groups there inevitably asked: (1) role of Communist Party in American movement (why doesn't it take leadership?); (2) role of trade unions (one guy tried to convince me it <u>had</u> to be in their interest to fight imperialism); and (3) role of black movement in the U.S. (will it join with the whites?). And others of interest: (1) what do you think of Cuba? (2) when do you think the war will end? and (3) what is the nature of the revolution in the North?

Wednesday, 25 October 1967, Vancouver (for 24 October 1967)

Trans-Pacific. And back to the "real world." The starkness of the real world hit me like a wet cold rag when I got on the plane and sized up the people on either side of me for conversation. To my left: chic, mod girl, San Francisco, back from Hong Kong. "When I went, I expected to see lots of dirty Chinese (shudder), but instead I saw so many handsome Caucasian men walking around the streets." To my right: young Filipino student of architecture, en route to Expo '67. "What do you think of the Huks?" [61] "They're bad. Shouldn't be allowed. U.S. must stay in Vietnam to prevent Communism from spreading in Asia." He was more flexible, as I learned after 2 hours of partially successful persuasion.

But, still, back to the white, rich West. The Filipino, at least, was indignant at what American GI's do to their women. Same reaction in Japan. An ugly thing, GI's have done—whored all the women. Even reactionaries probably hate them.

. . . Through the crazy International Date Line (left Tokyo Tuesday, 7:00 p.m., arrived Vancouver Tuesday, 11:00 a.m.). The North American continent again. Strange to be here. Miss Hanoi, but anxious to see American friends and test my knowledge, ability, effectiveness. And hastily finish writing before it passes.

Thursday, 26 October 1967 en route Regina

An attempt to sum up some information about military strategy, weapons, etc. (put together from observations, and questions with J.-P. Vigier, Ameri-

---

[61] Abbreviated term referring to a guerrilla force in the Philippines. Ronald E. Dolan, ed., *Philippines: A Country Study* (Washington, D.C.: Library of Congress, 1991), 362.

cans, Vietnamese). First, briefly, Vigier's analysis of where the war is: main distinction between U.S. and 3rd world has been scientific-technological. This contradiction is lessening as peoples' movements gain strength. First stage in Vietnam was U.S. "special war": providing weapons to national bourgeoisies which U.S. thought had popular support. This was a political failure. U.S. didn't reckon with forces of nationalism in the North, national and democratic bourgeois force in South, and national liberation (revolutionary) forces, (i.e., didn't expect revolution in 3rd world). The U.S. turned to stage 2, local warfare, using ground forces. This level now being lost. U.S. has had to escalate—and each stage has been anticipated by and prepared for by the Vietnamese. Heavy equipment and troops cannot be used on ground like Vietnam. But the first essential weapon is the ground forces—for the U.S.—and the infantry needs tanks. (Infantry increase is larger than that for planes.) The Vietnamese cannot be hit by "strategic surprise." U.S. tanks can't move through the jungle; when they try, they are met by large armament (such as shape charges). Guerillas also use walkie-talkies which intercept U.S. communication. The shifting point in the ground war was Junction City,[62] the U.S.'s last offensive. They tried to push back the population to the Cambodian border (presumably to capture NLF leadership). It was a fiasco: 2 brigades of the 1st Airborne Division were destroyed; many Americans destroyed by own planes—B-52 bombers; tanks moved too slowly and without success; air-dropped supplies were intercepted. (Don't know why the U.S. really planned this battle—but efforts were disastrous.) Now, since August 1967, over 8,000 men have been killed or wounded in the 17th parallel area (DMZ). There, Marines have been used (Con Thien), where they don't belong. Air support has dwindled, with 7th Fleet suffering. Forces have been spread over too wide a field. And every step of escalation swallows up more reserves. (Escalation is only useful when it results in quick victories.) The 2 U.S. "local war" offensives were 1965–1966 and 1966–1967, dry seasons, and investment mounted significantly: from 700,000 to 1 million troops, which included 200,000, then 410,000 Americans. Planes increased from 230,000 to 403,000. In 1954 to 1967, the U.S. budget in Vietnam has grown enormously:

---

[62] Operation Junction City took place in February 1967 in the area north of Saigon called the Iron Triangle. It was a large joint US-ARVN operation aimed at destroying the Central Office for South Vietnam, which was responsible for the Viet Cong guerrillas in the South. Young, *The Vietnam Wars*, 186.

- (1950–1954 $2.6 billion to France)
- 1954–1961 $1.6 billion
- 1961–1962 $2 billion
- 1965 $20 billion
- 1966 $24 billion
- 1967 $30 billion

And 200,000 are dead and wounded, compared to 20,000 in World War II. (Note: about ¼ of units are in actual fighting.) Raids of course have sky-rocketed: for example, in heavily bombed Quang Binh province, there were 3 raids in 1964, 1,985 in 1965, 14,000 in 1966.

In other words, in stage 2, the U.S. is trying to wage a war of attrition with small peoples against a people's war—and is failing.

Stage 3 is world war—commit genocide, or accept defeat—that is the contradiction. The Vietnamese expect the U.S. to increase the 17th parallel fighting, and intensify attacks all over the South. They expect increased bombing. They expect some genocidal tactics: crop destruction, for example. But they also are firm that the U.S. has lost, and will not, cannot, use an H-bomb.

U.S. presence in South Vietnam:
- 1950   35 people
- 1954   200
- 1960   3,000
- 1962   11,000
- 1964   30,000
- 1965   185,000
- 1966   383,000
- 1967   534,000
- in addition:
  - 7th Fleet   70,000
  - Thailand   35,000 (3 bases)
  - (South Korea and Australia)

What has been the U.S. response so far? The U.S. is being forced to change its target. Cities have become empty, because industry has been decentralized, and the population mobilized. So the remaining targets are bridges and roads, some of which are highly defended, such as Ham Lam Bridge. But another problem for the U.S. is bad weather, and bombing isn't always effective. First, process of bombing begins with <u>reconnaissance</u> planes which photograph a very high portion of the country daily. They must fly relatively low to get photos, and many have been lost. The time lag for photo development is at least ½ day and usually 1 day. Bomb sites are undoubtedly selected in Saigon. Then a plane goes out on a mission (sortie), from Thailand, 7th Fleet—maybe 800 sorties on a good clear day? Bombing is of 2 kinds. "Zone" bombing is terror bombing, done from high altitudes, with B-52s. An average trajectory is computed, and the bomb is aimed at the center of the square (target). Zone bombing is less dependent on the weather. "Precision" bombing is much more difficult: predetermined angles are set (it is highly computerized), for the plane "to get through" (under 200 meters) "the radar" (radar works unless there is "background"). Allowance must be made for the low cloud bank level, a stable formation. The plane must "dive" which puts it in the path of anti-aircraft or even rifles. There is only a little leeway in getaway—otherwise, the pilot can do little and has little time. For example, leaving the 7th Fleet, to Haiphong (18 km.) there are 3 seconds to adjust the bombs, etc. Therefore, many pilots "lob, hit, and run," especially over Haiphong and Hanoi. The U.S. has used some night-bombing, but in general it is inefficient and dangerous. Radar works at night, but planes can't see. On short passes it's "okay" and it has increased in Haiphong, but not in other places.

Few comments on actual weaponry. First, bombs and rockets are entirely different technologies, and changeover cannot be made easily. (China, for instance, has bombs, but not rockets.) The advantage of rockets is that they can be sent from a distance, further than bombs. Guided missile rockets (e.g., strike missiles) can actually be changed in course from the plane. Rockets, for example, could destroy the 7th Fleet (ground-to-ground; air-to-ground not fast enough), while it would take incredible tonnage of bombs to get a substantial amount of destruction—and the loss of planes would be fantastically high.

Planes themselves vary greatly in carrying capacity, use (cargo, bomber, fighter), flying altitude. In large use now are several 1950's planes which have been adapted for Vietnam. The F-105, originally high altitude nuclear bombing, now dives low in North Vietnam with iron bombs on its wings. This is no longer in production.

The F-4 (originally an interceptor) was Navy-developed, has had guns added to the nose to increase fighting ability with MIG's.

The B-52 is a strategic bomber (nuclear) which now carries iron bombs as a <u>tactical</u> plane. They are very costly, not very maneuverable, and fly very high to avoid being hit. (Also about 200 km/hour, slower than jet fighter bombers.)

The chief bomber in the South is the A-1, brought out of retirement—and no longer in production. Also in the South, slower planes like the B-52 can be used for weed killers (also in Laos), although slower planes are not needed for napalm or CBU's.

And of course there are helicopters, used for transporting troops and supplies, in the South.

It is difficult to know numbers of missions, loss of planes, etc. There is no question that the loss has increased. While in Vietnam, the tally was 2,397 on 15 October 1967—increased almost 70 in 2½ days. The U.S. says 687 planes in the North; and 775 fixed-wing aircraft in Vietnam (whole country? but mostly North). The Vietnamese claim loss of 1/100 planes. Too high? Don't have a way to resolve discrepancy, but in either case, the financial loss is staggering. Number of missions also varies—maybe 700 on a good day—maybe much less? Perhaps ¼ leave from Thailand, though more building is going on there now. The 7th Fleet, of course, is the essential element of the air war.

Some questions:
- Strafing: done a lot in the North: planes try to come in low, use bombs and automatic machine guns, for example, to hit convoys. How basic an element is this of the air war? (Low planes may escape radar and have accuracy, but also may burn up themselves with use of certain bombs.)
- How aware are pilots of the nature of their targets? In other words, do they know some are genocidal attacks? Vigier seemed to think not. Could be important for Nuremberg-type thoughts. Are they intentional murderers?? (Frequent path for pilot is Thailand to Laos to getaway to Guam.)
- Nature of Vietnamese camouflage? Vigier thinks it has many problems, especially trains.

Nature of air defense.
1. SAM's (surface to air missiles): very mobile, moved every night—countryside covered with holes for launching. They follow the heat of the plane and often are deadly (if they hit). Very high—up to 6 km. sometimes. They are radar-triggered. Sometimes a good pilot in a fast plane can outrun them.

2. <u>Middle range</u>: anti-aircraft. These are various machine guns, some light, some heavy. Also very mobile. Plane is spotted by radar, so defenders know its velocity and altitude. The anti-aircraft person computes where to shoot ahead of plane, or aims at plane on an angle (maximum distribution on the solid angle of the plane). In general, the Vietnamese don't use "general covering fire," too costly, and too revealing of position. They only shoot when fighting. Anti-aircraft reaches perhaps 3 km. high. Often arranged in ellipse-shape around target. (Often used to drive planes to levels where SAM's reach.)

3. <u>Low range</u>: rifle defense. Can be deadly when accurate. In general, it's important because it boosts morale and builds confidence to arm the population. And rifle-fire discourages low strafing, and pushes low planes up to level of anti-aircraft.

4. <u>Air</u>: MIG's. Small force (how many?) and not so effective, perhaps. But they boost morale. And they commit guerilla air tactics against U.S.—essentially a "pest" function that may interfere with U.S. missions.

30 October 1967, Monday, Regina

An attempted summary . . .

First, some observations on problems of the trip. I've mentioned most of these before, but will try to collect some thoughts. In retrospect, I do think all of us (except Tom) were woefully ill-prepared. We could have read a good deal more about Vietnam, about socialist societies. (Although on the other hand, I do believe it's hard to retain the information until you begin to use it.) But I think our skill at phrasing questions—even knowing which questions to ask—would've vastly improved if we'd done more preparation. The language problem is a different matter. Short of learning Vietnamese (which no Westerner <u>really</u> does well because of all the accents), one cannot avoid talking through an interpreter. That raises a variety of problems. First, learning to find out when the translator understands you and when he doesn't. Second, it's easy to talk to the translator rather than the non–English speaking person, instead of seeing the translator as a "means." In general conversation with several translators, it's easy to generalize to observations about the people and the society, from what is, after all, a mighty small sample! I dealt with this by trying to find non-verbal ways of gathering information: watching people's actions, expressions while talking, tone of their voice. Nevertheless, I was overwhelmed by the importance and frequent frustration I felt at not being able to communicate directly with people. (Also greatly increased my skepticism about reliability of journalists, etc., who write on the basis of interpretation-conversations.) There was also the milder problem of "behavior," wondering at times if we were doing the correct thing at the correct time. Somehow I don't think any of us flubbed too badly on this score—at least there were no visible signs.

Many of my thoughts (during and since the trip) have focused on the problem of understanding an alien culture and "what is truth?" Therein? To begin with, the country of Vietnam is alien on several levels: it is an Eastern country, with a different philosophical/religious tradition (the force of Buddhism, for example, or the "oriental" attitude towards life and death); it is a socialist society which make its structure, government, way of doing things quite unfamiliar; and perhaps hardest to comprehend, it is a society at war (and how strange this is to a mind and emotion which has experienced neither war nor a stage on constant revolution). It is impossible to conceive of constant expectation of death, yet everyone in Vietnam is well aware that in the next day, week, or month, the possibility of death for a close friend or relative is real. Within moments, an air alert may take people out to their defense posts—and bombs may fall. (Yet the irony is that often we were very shielded from the reality of the war, certainly from death.) It is possible for me to believe that the Vietnamese will continue the Revolutionary struggle till death; yet I cannot truly comprehend what inspires a people to do that. The truth is that the struggle for independence is literally woven into the blood and life-fabric of every man and woman of the country—people have matured in a society where struggle is ever-present. I see this, can explain it; but nothing in my own life-experience makes it real to me first-hand. Often, my reaction to this feeling was what I could only label humility, feeling there was a whole layer of every person there that could never be visible and comprehendible to me. The concept of "friendship" was, in this context, a difficult one: of course American peace people and Vietnamese could be friends, but truly on only a superficial level. That is, I think it is absurd to speak of us both in the same breath as revolutionaries. I don't want to suggest that the Americans are worthless and should be bathed in self-guilt; the fact simply is that our American "revolution" is a much lower-keyed, less-committed, and for most people, less a life-and-death struggle than what is (and has been) happening in Vietnam. And we have to be painfully aware of this in our speech and action.

What are some of the factors that make evaluation of Vietnam so very difficult? We approach any society with certain assumptions which stem quite legitimately from our own experiences as Americans and movement people. Yet these assumptions are not applicable to the very different Vietnamese society. First, for us, "government" means certain things. Historically we evolve from the Western liberal, bourgeois democratic tradition which views "government" as an administrative unit, quite different from what we consider "society." Western democracy grows from a tradition of monarchy; and it is society and not government that establishes mores, values, indeed, performs the basic function of socialization. Said differently, we see government and people as separate and distinct.

Yet the Vietnamese tradition is quite different. First, their government has no tradition of monarchy. Rather, they have been fighting colonialist foreign governments for centuries, and this molds the nature of their government. For the Vietnamese, government and people (society) are the same; the government is not simply an administrative implementer but rather a total structure that creates mores, values, etc. as well as implementing them.

A second problem is that of "individualism." The Western tradition is that people are private; first they are individuals and then members of a society, part of government, etc. Many assumptions flow from this: people act because of personal beliefs which of course differ for each, and it is not likely that all people would share the same goal. But we assume the primary importance of individualism, and whatever seems to sacrifice this is bad. That is, we assume all other societies must value individualism above all. And, I think, basically we often believe people won't sacrifice that individualism except under coercion.

Yet in Vietnam we are faced with a people who present an incredibly unified front, of belief in the struggle above all, whose individual personalities are merged, as it were, with the society's goals. And for a Westerner, the bells of suspicion, of distrust ring "Are they coerced? They can't really believe that . . . " Because people tell us the same thing, it is too easy to dismiss them. This is so hard to evaluate because individualism as an ethic is so deeply rooted in us. I think a couple of useful observations can be made. First, of course, people were different, and nothing suggested that we were being confronted with trained, robot-like people stamped from the same pattern. It is too easy to make that accusation based on language alone. (And of course things often sound the same, for reasons: problem of translation; interpreters knowing or at least using a rather standard English, especially the political terms; people telling us what they think they should rather than what they necessarily believe or prefer to say, particularly if they are officially representing the position of a mass organization.) People seemed to say different things, but more significantly, they said things differently. Manners, expressions, tones really varied a great deal, from young girls who giggled spontaneously, to rather dry bureaucrats, to people who spoke straight facts and data to those who spoke in parables (Mr. Ky, the journalist). It is true that in formal meetings styles were similar: presentation, list all questions, all questions answered (standard Communist Party operation, not at all peculiar to Vietnam). Yet where but in the movement is intellectual discussion so unordered and extemporaneous? This got buggy, but our own style would rile many a good, individualistic American university researcher or professor! Again, something triggers "suspicion," but not sure that is a valid response. I am sorry we didn't see more schools or more young people. There I suspect we would find a lot of variety and "individualism."

I've also thought about this problem in terms of "socialization." Vietnamese socialization perhaps takes the form of unifying people in support of struggle for the fatherland. People are socialized to be patriotic and united. Perhaps it is because we (especially movement people) see government as the enemy, that we cannot really accept people for their government as genuine and non-coerced. But it is simple, a matter of a different socialization process—perhaps we should examine socialization itself! Americans are socialized, but not to be patriots, instead, to be consumers (what else is the effect of the TV's, billboards, etc. that surround us with their insidious messages?). We might wonder if it's different for people in the movement: do we have an identity above our own individualism? Even for most of us, I think, personal fulfillment comes first, above the goals of the movement, when the two clash. Yet to many Americans, we all look and sound the same—observers do not trust us, think our reactions are not genuinely self-inspired. We just see a somewhat similar force in an entire society in Vietnam, and this grates, because we are accustomed to being a minority.

There is a related, but slightly different problem: that of coercion, control. Again, Westerners are suspicious when they hear what they believe is a "line," for this spells coercion. I got itchy as I was told, repeatedly, that people distinguish between peace-loving Americans and American aggressors. Or when people talked in non-personal terms. Yet the situation is so so different: they are at war, they are talking not only to foreigners, but to Americans! They are, perhaps, official bureaucrats of sorts; and finally, they do believe in the struggle against the Americans and in the need to sacrifice for the struggle for that is part of their basic tradition.

These are but a few problems . . .

Now, want to try to sketch several of the main impressions I had, and put them into the context of the terribly difficult problem of explanation of all this. The previous thoughts are problems I've felt with my own thinking and reacting; but even more, how does all this get explained to someone who hasn't been to Vietnam. How do we communicate the need to throw off our own assumptions about our own society to "step into" Vietnam on their terms? After all, we are children of our own society. (Thinking here of the problem other left-wing people had after trips to the Soviet Union, for example.) What things can be said, how to most clearly explain Vietnam.

One might argue about the "two realities of Vietnam," the reality of the war and the reality of the new society they are building. It is the latter, of course, that is so difficult for us to comprehend (again, those Western "suspicions"). The truth appears to be that the Vietnamese are constructing a revolutionary society which is intertwined with their fighting a war. There is a tremendous surge forward occurring, even faster, perhaps, then they expected. For example, they learn that creation of a health center in reality takes 12 months, not the planned 2 years. There are signs all over that the population is fantastically mobilized, for fighting and to achieve progress. Thus, it is not rare to find the young girl we did, employed in an underground factory (rifle by her side) at a lathe making axles, who works overtime "for my country." (Patriotism and spirit truly abound.) Progress exists technologically, but curiously, we are surprised by this—we persist in remarking with wonder at the ingenuity of a "society on bicycles." (How similarly did Europe react to the advance of the immature Revolutionary American society?) But energy is massive, and is being fruitfully harnessed. Many striking examples of such growth, some of course induced by the conditions of war: hospitals are totally mobile in the countryside, with the bicycle-turned generators; new foods and medicines have been developed (e.g., fish powder); agricultural innovations have developed. (Everything has been turned into a factory in Hanoi!)

But more fascinating are the social and human innovations, improvisations, arrangements that are occurring in the society. The war has necessitated dispersal to the countryside of children, schools, and factories. Initially a hardship, the Vietnamese are learning about possible new relationships between city and country, which might relieve the rural-urban tensions most societies experience. Women have taken a new role in production and agriculture and, as a result, their role in the entire society is shifting. The "unit principle" of fighting is applied informally to all kinds of work, which means everyone participates in some form of social organization. Because of the dependency, in the countryside, of air defense on the peasants (no radar, communication often is verbal), each person is given an important role and stake in what happens. Everyone counts, so to speak.

31 October 1967, Tuesday, en route

Many social arrangements have occurred in the fields of education and public health: the need to mobilize the population preventively has been crucial. In education, wipe out illiteracy and in public health prevent disease (wipe out epidemics), to keep the population prepared. In both fields, many local people have been involved in creating these structures. What I found significant was the stress on population mobilization preventively, made necessary by the war. (Can we speak of "guerilla tactics" for wiping out illiteracy and epidemics?) Another major "arrangement" is the high degree of decentralization, critical in many respects. Initially, problems of communication, transportation, and varied conditions from province to province make impossible a highly centralized apparatus. Thus, implementation of many programs (and much decision-making) occurs on the local level. Results have been beneficial: locally, people left to their own ingenuity and resources have produced well; and I suspect a variety of thought, culture, etc. is being well-preserved and valued. The Vietnamese value differences, a lot of emphasis is placed on the ethnic minorities, on getting people to appreciate others' traditions in the country. Probably stems from a realistic assessment of attitudes but nevertheless has a positive effect.

There are some critically important attitudes I should try to spell out. First, the attitude towards time. It seems to me that the Vietnamese have a remarkably flexible plasticity about time. They expect progress to come from constant improvisation, from adapting whatever is available to their own purposes. Yet they also have a patience. They certainly believe in progress, in fact everything is utilized to bring about progress. But they are not chauvinistic about Vietnam on this score. Rather, they are most willing to borrow and adapt any and all resources. Thus, they are eager to admit their possession of Czech machines, French bicycles ("we've looked around and bought up the best bicycles in the world"), and Walt Disney cartoon devices ("he was a political reactionary but had a genius for cartoon"). They rely enormously on inventive and improvising abilities of their own people; and they ignore no resources. Everything and everyone is seen as an element of possible change.

Thus, it is no wonder that they see their own destiny being molded in their own hands. The agency of change is their own people. They do not view themselves as the object of American intentions, militarily, or prey to the technological status of America (and doomed, therefore, to inferior status).

The American "world-view" is of technologically advanced countries whose faith is that the future comes from constant planning, and small backward countries. The former can "offer" its technology to these countries, and their job is to be "good missionaries." Furthermore, Vietnam now suffers greatly as the object of the American war. What happens there is the result of American success or failure; very little regard is paid to the strength of the Vietnamese as their own agents. All of U.S. policy is based on these attitudes. For example, Diem fell partly because the U.S. didn't convince the peasants that the Communists were bad, not because peasants supported the "Viet Cong."

3 November 1967, Friday, Boston

More, on the problem of time. Vietnamese attitude towards time is one of the most important, I believe,—so I keep going back to try to approach the question in different ways. I've said I think it is flexible, with an importance on improvisation. There are important implications for behavior. That is, it seemed to me that behavior is well integrated—that people in the society, under severe crisis, nevertheless operate well. Which is not to say people just live for the present. But they deal well with the immediate present, plan for the future as they can, but are infinitely adaptable in the present because of the war. There is recognition as well that continuity in the society can develop from the least expected places—that is, there is a fluidity within the society, and continuity and growth seem to stem more from applying principles of growth to existing resources than from step-by-step plans. Hard to articulate. Western change is stage by stage, as technology unfolds (so many people believe); Vietnamese emphasis is on change wherever it's found, and no great faith in "the" plan, although of course the socialist ideology does suggest certain paths of development.

Attitudes about time are reflected in attitudes about the length of the war. When do people think it will end? I was struck, especially, by the attitude of the youth. They have grown up with war and struggle around them except for a few peaceful years. Their "adjustment" is remarkable—they seem to have found ways to carry on "normal" existences, with some room for love, play, study, work, despite the war. They have not lived through a time of ". . . remember when" whose memories might embitter them. I truly found the young people so open and spontaneous, and happy in appearance. In contrast the people who showed the strain were the older people, especially peasant women (who, perhaps, show the strain worldwide), who are simply tired of fighting. The people harder to describe are the 40 yr olds—many of whom were soldiers in the French resistance and don't fight now. They expect the war to end, but they have the bitter experience of fighting for independence and a peace which has been rudely interrupted. I'm speaking here of men like Oanh, or Nguyen Minh, somewhat established people, who take a firm ideological position about the war ending, but I really can't characterize their attitudes and expectations. Maybe 5 years at the most? Maybe another year at the least?

The youth, I think, expect the war to end and look forward to and speak of the future. Yet I think they have a real pride in fighting—a staggering patriotism. Their fighting—eagerness to join the army—is not unlike the determined eagerness of youth Negro "troops" in the South who expected violence.

Thoughts about emotion and sentimentality.

Many people have asked me questions about the Vietnamese as "real people," for examples of personal contact. I think this is a tough thing to generalize about. I reacted negatively to Hayden and Lynd's attempts to speak about the "Vietnamese people" based only on intimate contact with a few people.[63] The word often used to describe the Vietnamese is sentimental, an incorrect word I think. "Passionate" is perhaps more appropriate. But this is also a problem of a strange culture. The Vietnamese have different emotional complexions than we do in the West. We here know the common example of "men are not supposed to cry." Perhaps Vietnamese show emotions differently. That is, we are trained to look for and to exhibit certain responses at certain times. In formal situations, or particularly in political situations when we are trying to present a "front," we seem

---

[63] A Yale professor, Staughton Lynd traveled to North Vietnam with Tom Hayden and Herbert Aptheker, an American communist, in 1965. There they met with an American prisoner of war held in Hanoi. Staughton Lynd and Tom Hayden, *The Other Side* (New York: Signet Books, 1967).

different than when we're eating or loving. In general, the Vietnamese we met were in the former situation of presenting a front to us, and we couldn't expect the casualness of a long-time friendship. This describes 2 problems for me. One is the question of "individualism." We met individuals, true, but in their organization capacity. And while I spent much time alone with Peace Committee people, I am reluctant to generalize. How representative are they? Oanh, for one, is very Western in some ways. All of them are what we'd call middle-class organizational people—a far cry from being peasants, though Oanh did come from a workers' family near Haiphong and Hieu from Saigon. My own sense is that I saw lots of differences from man to man and woman to woman—voice inflections, facial expressions, gestures, varied greatly. (How often has the Left been accused of sounding and looking the same—the pervasive New Left style!)

The second issue is that of emotion, of people as humans rather than in their official capacity. I got easily suspicious of kids talking about American friends vs. American aggressors. I wanted to scream "you should hate us"—guilt helplessly rises. But perhaps their hatred is used differently. That is, we are socialized to show hatred one way, usually externalized. But perhaps the Vietnamese are socialized to deal with hatred by internalizing it; that is, the incredible hatred of Americans which I don't, for a moment, doubt the existence of, could be a potentially destructive force. But they have learned to harness that hatred and use it productively, to fight harder, to strengthen the determination which they do show. It is no accident that hatred of the U.S. makes men Viet Cong, that American military policy breeds communism, as it were. I sensed this over and over. There are symbols, too. For example, Phu Ka village, leveled by the U.S., has erected a "hatred house," (i.e., museum), a constant reminder of what happened and what perhaps might happen again if people don't resist successfully. In addition, perhaps we can interpret the whole business of the distinction between friends and aggressors as giving people a chance to vent full-blown hatred against the aggressors. So it is not necessary for the Vietnamese to hate American friends; because liking us strengthens the contrasting feeling of hatred for them, for the enemy.

(Need to do more thinking on this, the whole psychology of what, after all, is a pretty standard communist line.)

The other part of the question is how people show emotions. Several real-life examples come to mind. First, the night of the Song and Dance House performance, when several Peace Committee people brought their kids. The whole image of the robot-like mass organization man with total political discipline (etc.) got greatly softened. Who could react that way, seeing a man with a little kid clawing at his trouser legs? There were also many things said—innuendos, signs of affection, characteristic of the Vietnamese people and very, very human. I would guess that many exchanges were male-female though it's hard to tell. Mine were simply because no females were around full-time as our hosts. But on one occasion, an American gave a flowery speech about "leaving part of his heart with the Vietnamese." Hieu turned to me, smilingly, and said, a twinkle in his eye, "I'd much rather have a piece of your heart." In retrospect, that's both a warm personal statement and interestingly, also, an indication of an emotional choice. The Vietnamese are careful to not take sides, to not show preferences, but there was enough teasing of this sort to be very "human." Another example: at a banquet, with everyone a bit cheerful and a bit high, one of the Vietnamese requested that I give a toast and challenge one of the Americans and one of the Vietnamese to "bottoms up." I did. The Vietnamese downed the liqueur; the American didn't; and the Vietnamese proceeded to tease him. Aside from the suggestion that the Vietnamese may be laughing at the Americans about the whole drinking, who-can-take-it business, the very fact that they do that, and in fine humor, breaks the image of tight political actors. They may think they are "taking" us, but their willingness to indulge in such sport (and I really had the feeling they considered it sport) was very human. Or, better said, it left me with impressions of them as individuals in social situations, impressions I cherish.

Briefly, on a totally different point, about "socialist realism." I disliked much of it. I wasn't greatly inspired by the cartoons, I was a little bored with the morality of some of the films, though I thought Nguyen Van Troi was excellent. But several discussions since have created in me more appreciation, or at least more sympathy, for such a style. I was thinking of the effect of French (or any other colonial presence anywhere) education, culture, in Vietnam. How would a Vietnamese kid react, for example, to French poems about flowers and trees and constellations in the sky he never sees, or tales about kids and their domestic animals, or stories about French industrialization? I'm not speaking of history; I'm speaking of assumed cultural, natural traditions (analogous to black kids seeing white story books which assume whiteness and little-box suburbs as the norm). The presence of foreign cultures (probably more dramatic with the English teaching Wordsworth and Shelley to Indians, Africans, and even Australians!) is so alien, so far from the local population's experience, and so confusing, that it is not too surprising to see the emergence of an almost fanatical insistence on accuracy, true portrayal, and all that. Norm's account of realism in films is an extreme: if a film about good rice is being bad, a bad harvest cannot be photographed as a good one; the film-maker would have to wait for the next good crop. But they do not want attempts at "true films" rather than fiction to conflict with the actual experience people have.

[The narrative entries of Carol McEldowney's Hanoi journal end here. The last section of the journal contains a collection of notes, lists, and illustrations about the trip.]

Chao (Tam Biet): good-bye
Không dám (q-h'ong zam): don't mention it
Dông Cho: comrade
Các Mác: Karl Marx
chấo bác: greetings (older man or woman) (bac = uncle)
chấo co: greetings (younger person)
chấo chi: greetings (same age)
chấo ban: greetings, friend
can bo: cadre
có khoě khóng (k'where(e) k'ong): how are you?
    ban cố . . . friend
    ông cố . . . old man
    anh cố . . . man
    chi cố . . . sister
    bác cố . . . old person
dep lăm: beautiful
ten thi (anh) la de?: how old are you (male)?
khoě lăm: well (bien) [cám ỏn khoě lắm: thank you I'm well]
cám ỏn (an): thank you
có: yes
không: no (or not)
ban: friend; chao các ban: greetings, friends!
mỹ (mae): American
may bay mỹ: American plane

hōa bīnh (hua bing): peace
giải phóng (zai fong): liberation
dôc lâp (dock lup): independence

chúc ban khoe (wquá): go well
hùữ nghi (huy ñāy): friendship
tên chi (anh) lā gí (ze): what is your name? (male)
tên tôo lá _____ (ten toy la): my name is _____

có lảm ỏn: please
có lảm ỏn cho tôi xin: please give me
   . . . tỏ giay (to zay): . . . paper
   . . . thuốc lá: . . . cigarette
sủa chủa: yogurt (sour milk)
sủa ca-cảo: milk with cocoa
ca phê sủa: coffee with milk
ca phê den: coffee (black)
ca phê phin: coffee filtered
ca phê da: iced coffee
ché da: iced tea
bia: beer
nước chanh: lemonade
chuâi (chew-ā): banana

Miscellaneous Culture, Social, Etc.

Village organization:
   Hamlets (200–400 households)
   (agricultural cooperative at hamlet level)
   can be several cooperatives within one village

Money:
   100 sau = 1 dong
   3.5 dong = $1.00
   1 dong = 28.5 cents
   50 sau = c. 15 cents
   25 sau = c. 7½ cents

Ket doan: Unity song, originally a Chinese tune

Xunhasaba: import-export house. Canadian distribution: Book World, 72 Gerrand Street West, Toronto 2, Ontario; and Progress Books, 487 Adelaide St. West, Toronto 2B, Ontario, Canada.

Ket Đoan

ket đoan chung ta là suc manh
Ket đoan chung ta là sat gang
Doan ket ta ben vung
Du sat hay là gang
Ma sat hay gang con Kem ben Vung
Chung ta the pha tan quân thu
Thuc dan de quoc sai Lang
nôi voi phe phan đong
ta đấp tan hoang
Tien tien mau mau cò tu do.
Lang reo vôn trong anh duong
Xay đoi moi theo dan
chu moi

Unity   Kết Đoàn

United, we shall have strength
United, we shall be steel
United, we could be firm.
Even iron and steel
Couldn't be firmer than us
We pledge to defeat the enemy,
~~Be the~~ colonialists, imperialists,
and the reactionary clique
We will defeat them
Let's ~~advance~~ march forward
Freedom is coming to meet us
under the sunlight
We will build a new life
in new democracy /.

KẾT ĐOÀN

"Ket Đoan—Unity Song" lyrics and music (not in McEldowney's handwriting).

Population: North, 18 million, ethnic minorities
South, 16 million: Thai Mao, 330,000; Buddhists, 13 million; Viet-Bac, 800,000

Hectare: 2½ acres

Kết đoàn [not in McEldowney's handwriting]

Kết đoàn chung ta la suc manh
Kết đoàn chung ta la sat gang
Doan ket ta ben vung
Du sat hay la gang
Ma sat hay gang con kem ben vung
Chung ta the pha tan quân thu
Thuc dan đe quoc sai lang voi phe phan đong ta đâp tan hoang
Tien tien mau mau co tu do
Đang reo von trong anh duong
Xay doi moi theo dan chu moi

[Translation and music were stapled onto the adjacent page.]
Unity (Kết Đoàn) [not in McEldowney's handwriting]

United, we shall have strength
United, we shall be steel
United, we could be firm.
Even iron and steel
Couldn't be firmer than us
We pledge to defeat the enemy, colonialists, imperialists, and the
    revolutionary clique
We will defeat them
Let's march forward
Freedom is coming to meet us under the sunlight
We will build a new life in new democracy
Kết Đoàn

April, 1965, <u>Four Points</u>: response to American aggression; ignored by
United States
  1. recognition of national rights of Vietnamese people; withdrawal of
     U.S. troops and cessation of bombing

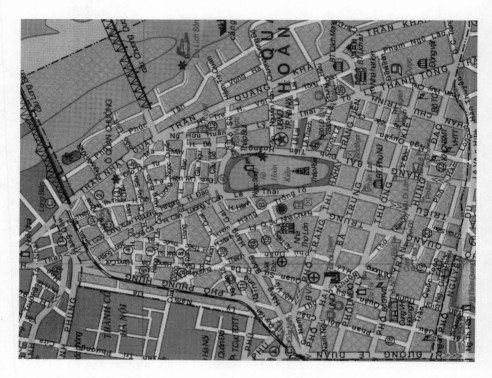

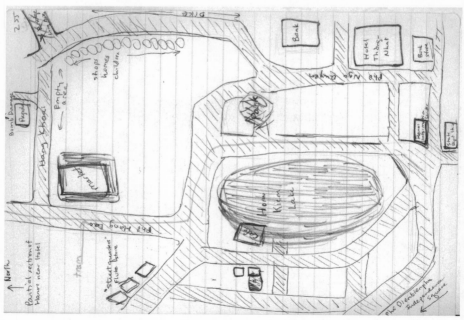

2. respect for military provisions of Geneva Agreements: no military alliances
3. South Vietnamese, under NLF, settle own internal affairs
4. peaceful reunification settled by Vietnamese people

Key Events and Places

Mu Gia: site of first bombing, near Laotian border

Phat Diem: large Catholic center, important fishing center, famous handicrafts center. Destroyed by bombing April 1966ff.

Thanh Hoa: heavily bombed province. Has Tinh Gia district: important communications center. Model village in spite of bombing. Ham Rong bridge (very defended) at Thanh Hoa. TB Hospital.

Nam Dinh: third largest city of DRV; south of Hanoi; heavily bombed

Indochinese Communist Party: formed 3 February 1930

Yen Phuc: village near Ham Rong bridge, badly bombed

Quang Binh Province: near 17th parallel, very heavy bombing

Nghe An Province: Quynh Lap leprosy hospital bombed

Paul Doumer Bridge: across Red River, joins Hanoi with (Long Bien) Gia Lam suburb. Bombed August 1967

5 August 1964: Gulf of Tonkin

2 March 1965: first non-retaliatory raids on North and beginning of systematic bombing of North.

Organizations

Lao Dong: Communist (Workers' Party) Party of DRV; formed after Communist Party of Indochina dissolved. "Great Four" leaders: Truong Chinh, Ho Chi Minh, Vo Nguyen Giap, Pham Van Dong

FACING PAGE

LEFT: *Sketch map of hotel's Hanoi neighborhood.*

RIGHT: *Modern map of Hanoi, neighborhood detail (courtesy Nguyen Ba Chung).*

Women's Union: "3 Responsibilities" movement:
1. replace men in all work so they can fight
2. care for family and encourage men to fight
3. fight whenever necessary

"Three-Readies Movement" of Youth:
1. ready to fight valiantly and enlist in army
2. ready to overcome all problems, and stimulate work and studies
3. go anywhere needed by Motherland

Phai Doan Dai Dân, Mat Tran Dan Toc Giai Phong
Mien Nam Viet Nam: permanent representative of NLF

Vietnam Federation of Trade Unions: Presidium
President: Hoang Quoc Viet (chairman)
General Secretary (Secretariat): Tran Danh Tuyen, Vice-Chairman
Auditing Commission (Chairman): Nguyen Long Hòa, Vice-Chairman

Fatherland Front: established September 1955. Born of Viet Minh (1941)
Front (League for Independence) and Lien Viet (1946) Front (League of
Vietnamese People): The Front.

NLF Mission, Hanoi
Mr. Tien
Mr. Tran Van Hieu

Vietnam Committee for the Defense of World Peace
68 Ly Thuong Kiet St.
Hanoi DRV
Cable address: Vietpeace Hanoi
Nguyen Trung Hieu

Peace Committee
Ha Huy Tam (interpreter)
Nguyen Khoa Toan (typist)
Dang Thai Toan (? No French, English)

DRV; V. Tisine 2; Praha 6

Khach San Thống-Nhất
Phô Ngo Quyen, Hanoi

A–D

Pham Van Bach: President of DRV Supreme Court, Vice-President of Vietnam Jurists' Association

Ta Quang Buu: Minister of Higher Education. Signer of Geneva Agreements.

Phan Thi An: Women's Union

Major Bai: Army, in charge of U.S. pilots

Le Duan: First Secretary, Central (Executive) Committee of Lao Dong

Tran Van Dinh: South Vietnam ambassador to U.S. until Diem regime fell. "Friend" of Buddhists. Lives in Washington, writes for New Republic.

Truong Chinh: author of principles for "Long war." One of four founders of I.C.P., important in Lao Dong. Leading political theorist.

Pham Van Dong: also trained in Canton with Ho; organized underground trade union movement. Back in Vietnam 1940. Prime Minister.

Nguyen Thi Dinh: female deputy chief of South Liberation Army

E–H

Hoang Van Hoan: Vice Chairman of DRV National Assembly Standing Committee

Vo Nguyen Giap: head of army, Defense Minister, and important thinker. Chief general at Dien Bien Phu.

Nguyen Van Huyen: Minster of Education, developing educational system to meet the bombing

Nguyen Van Hieu: NLF Representative to Phnom Penh, formerly to Prague. Also general secretary of Association of Patriotic Journalists of South Vietnam, 53, Samdech Pann, Phnom Penh, Cambodge.

Thu Hường: "Hanoi Hannah"

Pham Hong: (a) secretary of Peace Committee (at Bratislava)

Nguyen Trung Hieu: interpreter for Peace Committee (Chi, Hieu)

J–M

Ho Chi Minh: (Nguyen Ai Quoc) formed:
   League of Colonial Countries (post WWI)*
   League of Oppressed People of Asia (from Canton, 1920s)*
   Vietnamese Association for Mutual Assistance (Thailand, circa 1928)*
   Vietnam Independence League (Vietminh, 1941)
   (Also, League of Revolutionary Vietnamese Youth, 1920s)
      *3 February 1930 Communist Party of Indochina.

Colonel Ha Van Laû: secretary, standing member of War Crimes Investigation Committee

Tran Làm: editor-in-chief of Voice of Vietnam

Mr. Ky: Journalists' Association

Nguyen Minh: secretariat member (one of eight) of Vietnam Federation of Trade Unions

Le Mai: c/o Permanent Mission of South Vietnam NLF; Prague c/o 20 San-Li-Tun;
   Moscow   Peking
   Budapest   P.R.C.

N–Q

Le Thanh Nghi: Central Committee of Workers' Party, Political Bureau, member; Vice Premier

R–U

Mr. Tien: NLF Representative to the DRV

Ton Duc Thang: Central Committee of Vietnam Fatherland Front

Nguyen Van Troi: martyred hero of the South; a young electrician who was executed for his activities, 1964, for trying to kill McNamara. Has become national hero.

Pham Van Que: DRV ambassador to Prague

Dr. Pham Ngoc Thach: minister of Public Health

Pham Huy Thong: Director of Pedagogic Institute, historian

Doan Trong Truyen: a key figure in State Planning Committee

Nguyen Duy Trinh: Foreign Minister. Important interview with Burchett, 29 January 1967 about negotiations.

V–Z

Mr. Hoang Quoc Viet: head of trade unions, and high DRV position (Vietnam General Confederation of Labor)

General Nguyen Van Vinh: assistant chief-of-staff of VPA. Chairman of Committee for Re-unification. Military theoretician.

Nguyen Minh Vy: head of DRV delegation at Bratislava. Gave important speech at Stockholm.

Schedule in Vietnam

Saturday, September 30
  early morning; drive around city: One Pillar Pagoda, Unity Park
  meeting to plan program
  afternoon: Museum of the Vietnamese People's Army
  evening: banquet; documentary films

Sunday, October 1
  6 a.m.: Museum of the Revolution
  afternoon: tailor
  evening: Song and Dance Ensemble

Monday, October 2
  a.m.: Hanoi War Crimes Tribunal Committee; bomb damage, seven
    schools
  afternoon: meeting with Committee; bomb damage: Pho Hue, Pho Mai
    Hac De, Hoan Kiem hospital, Phu Xa
  evening: walk, Hanoi Information Center

Tuesday, October 3
  a.m.: evacuated factory
  afternoon: Trade Union Federation

Wednesday, October 4
  a.m.: Pham Ngoc Thach, Pham Van Bach, Ha Van Lau
  afternoon: Hanoi Surgical Hospital: medical report, bomb victims;
    International Press Club: Ministry of Education on school bombings
  evening: National War Crimes Tribunal: weapons exhibition

Thursday, October 5
a.m.: prepare for province trip; visit handicraft stores
4 p.m.: leave for Nam Ha Province; visit Phu Le on route
evening: official meeting, Nam Ha

Friday, October 6
a.m.: official meeting; walk around; see American plane
afternoon: local entertainment; more meetings; trip: evacuated part of
Nam Dinh hospital; Nam Dinh: Pho Hang Thao, Pho Hoang Van
Thu; underground factory; night school

Saturday, October 7
(a.m.: long air alert)
afternoon: Hanoi mayor
evening: Women's Union; film from GDR

Sunday, October 8
a.m.: Museum of Arts and Handicrafts
afternoon: Mr. Vy, Thong Nhat
evening: meet with VPA about seeing pilots

Monday, October 9
a.m.: trip to Dan Phuong Agricultural Cooperative

Tuesday, October 10
afternoon: Committee on Cultural Relations with Foreign Countries;
films: dances, Nguyen can Troi
late dinner and walk

Wednesday, October 11
morning walk
a.m.: Museum of Revolution to see Dien Bien Phu film
afternoon: Mr. Ky, Journalists' Association
evening: meeting with intellectuals

Thursday, October 12
a.m.: Voice of Vietnam; Premier Pham Van Dong
afternoon: Voice of Vietnam tapes
evening: see American pilots

Friday, October 13
a.m.: Xunhasaba (export-import)
noon: banquet

afternoon: article for and interview with Thong Nhat
evening: long walk

Saturday, October 14
a.m., 3 p.m.: meetings with Peace Committee
evening: National Library, and walk

Sunday, October 15
morning: walk
afternoon: talk with John Pierre Vigier
evening: talk with Nguyen Minh

Monday, October 16
a.m.: Voice of Vietnam, propaganda plans; tape with "Hanoi Hannah"
evening: visit night schools

Tuesday, October 17
Drive around Hanoi; cartoon studio